NEW POETRY OF NEW ENGLAND

FROST AND ROBINSON

LONDON: HUMPHREY MILFORD

OXFORD UNIVERSITY PRESS

NEW POETRY OF NEW ENGLAND

FROST AND ROBINSON

By

ROBERT P. TRISTRAM COFFIN

BALTIMORE

THE JOHNS HOPKINS PRESS

1938

PRINTED IN THE UNITED STATES OF AMERICA
BY J. H. FURST COMPANY, BALTIMORE, MARYLAND

1 6 6 11

To

BAYARD AND MARGARET TURNBULL

WHO MADE THESE LECTURES

A LOVELY MILESTONE

IN MY LIFE

ACKNOWLEDGMENTS

The author is greatly indebted to Henry Holt and Company, for permission to reprint material from *Collected Poems* and *A Further Range* by Robert Frost; and to The Macmillan Company for permission to quote from *Collected Poems* of Edwin Arlington Robinson, from *The Song of Honour* of Ralph Hodgson, and from the author's own books, *Golden Falcon, The Yoke of Thunder,* and *Strange Holiness.*

To Robert Frost the author owes a tremendous debt of gratitude, not only for his kindness in permitting his poems to be reprinted, but for his extraordinary kindness in so generously helping, by letters and advice, to make these lectures possible.

ROBERT P. TRISTRAM COFFIN.

FOREWORD

In 1889 Mr. and Mrs. Lawrence Turnbull of Baltimore established in honor of their son, Percy Graeme, who had died in 1887, a foundation for lectures on poetry to be delivered at The Johns Hopkins University and to be called the Percy Turnbull Memorial Lectureship. Thirty-four series of lectures have been given. R. C. Jebb, Charles Eliot Norton, Ferdinand Brunetière, Henry Van Dyke, Menéndez Pidal, G. L. Kittredge, Emile Legouis, "Æ," T. S. Eliot, Lascelles Abercrombie, and H. J. C. Grierson have been among the speakers. This year we were fortunate in having a penetrating interpretation of New England poetry from one who is, by birth, training, and residence, a New Englander to the core, as well as a distinguished poet and student of poetry. The warm appreciation that his lectures received made it appropriate that they should reach, by publication, a much larger audience. Mr. Coffin's manuscript, generously presented by him to the Lectureship, is consequently now made accessible to the public. It is hoped that readers may grasp, under his guidance, the pathos of verses inspired by the decay of much that was fine in New England life and may find, as do Frost and Coffin, the new joy that comes from a deepened appreciation of nature in its varied aspects and from a keener insight into the hearts of men.

H. Carrington Lancaster
Chairman of the Lecture Committee

The Johns Hopkins University
May 5, 1938

CONTENTS

INTRODUCTION

I want to say first of all, before I begin on my subject of *New Poetry of New England*, that I appreciate deeply the great honor paid me in your invitation to join the very distinguished fellowship of my predecessors in the Percy Turnbull Memorial Lectureship in Poetry. I feel somewhat as my master Geoffrey Chaucer felt at the end of his greatest poem, *Troilus and Criseyde*. As he made his obeisance to Homer, Virgil, Lucan, and Statius, so I make mine to E. C. Stedman, Charles Eliot Norton, the poet "Æ.," my old teacher, Sir Walter Raleigh, George Lyman Kittredge, Mr. Lascelles Abercrombie, and Professor Herbert J. C. Grierson.

I feel especially humble, because I am not really a scholar of poetry at all. I was once, for a few years at Oxford. And I sometimes wish that I might have gone on being one. But I have been too busy being a maker of poetry myself. A man has only so many days in a year and so many years in a lifetime. Such time as I could spare from the teaching of poetry, I have spent in the creation of more. Poetry has been my avocation, and it has cut, not only into my hours of sleep and ephemeral exercise, but also into those hours I might have spent in critical research. I have used the third watch of the night for my making of poetry, for many years now. That is the time when the barnyard timekeeper of the night feels the sun slip over the bottom surface of the earth below his roost and start on its upward way. I find that time the best for living over again the excitements of expe-

rience and inspiration in a calmer mood—which I take to
be one of the liveliest definitions of poetry, even though
it is Wordsworth's and over a century old. In these hours
of quiet, a man feels most alone, on the face of the sleeping world, and in his watchful loneliness he takes over
some certain powers in the universe, and becomes, as it
were, a deputy of divinity. Then it is he seems to be more
easily in touch with the slenderer vibrations of life, often
obscured in the day, which, in spite of all that science has
yet told us, may come from sources outside our world,
making their way like winged seeds of cosmic life, sailing
across the wide meadows where the stars and nebulae
blossom.

I have dwelt thus at length on my avocation of poetry,
because, it seems to me, the fact of my being a poet may
well give me some authority to talk critically about it and
justify my standing here this afternoon in a famous university as a lecturer in a famous lectureship. If I have not
analyzed as much as some other men, I have created material somewhat akin to that which they have taken apart.
It may be that the process of putting poems together has
developed in me some powers which are not possessed by
the scholars of poetry. I hope so, for your sakes.

I should have ventured upon very dubious ground indeed, if I had chosen for my subject that segment of the
rainbow of English poetry which I examined closely as a
scholar of Oxford, the early seventeenth century, Milton,
and especially the work of John Donne, Dean of Paul's,
and the metaphysical-religious poets who went to school
to him. For that particular period has been discussed by

at least two of your more recent lecturers, Mr. T. S. Eliot and that leading metaphysical authority, the brilliant Professor Grierson of the University of Edinburgh. One can have enough of a good thing. Though I had something new to say, your patience could hardly be expected to bear another series of lectures on the seventeenth century!

I have taken some pains to choose a subject suited to me. I am, as I have said, something of a poet, I think; and I *know* I am a New Englander, by birth, by education, and by residence. I know the people and the hills and the weather north of Boston, and hence I may be able to give you something new in my discussion of the poetry of New England, during these weeks. Maybe, I shall be able to present a study possessing more unity than otherwise, even if it is only the unity of a poet's mind. At any rate, I shall be speaking as a native on a native subject. I did not attend Harvard, but I did attend a college that has something of the older New England academic virtues and, like Harvard, a double set of governing boards, both Overseers and Trustees, if that is any virtue. So maybe my academic foundation is sound. My college, Bowdoin, also has produced two of the greatest of the older New England writers, the poet Longfellow and the story-teller Hawthorne; and as a Bowdoin man, therefore, I speak in a literary tradition. Both of the poets whose work will largely make up my matter are New Englanders from north of Boston. One indeed was from Maine, a Kennebec man, with the Kennebec's loveliness built into his stanzas; and the other, though he has lived the best of his life in New Hampshire and Vermont, has ancestors that hailed from Maine, and has written about the kind of people and places I know best. So as a New Englander, as a northern New Englander, as a Maine man, and as a poet, I ought to be at home in my subject. And in closing this apology, I should like to ask you to believe that when, on three or four occasions, I shall quote from my own poems, it is for the sake of an exposition of my theme rather than for an exposition of my own power as a poet.

THE WORLD THAT IS GONE

There are many writers, at the moment, in New England. There is a whole school of Maine novelists, for instance, who have something of the sparkle and the freshness of that wellspring of native Maine beauty, Sarah Orne Jewett. But I must, of course, limit myself to poets. There are several of them in Maine and many in New England. With my corner of the land, it is as it is with kings. The king is dead, long live the king! Just at the moment, when the rest of the country was relegating New England poetry to the company of the ancient dead, putting Bryant and Longfellow, Whittier and Holmes and Lowell safely away into libraries and text-books, a whole new brood of New England poets broke their shells and came out into the cold clear light of Boston and Derry and Burlington and Cambridge, piping a new kind of music. We had had Romanticists and Transcendentalists, and now we had Imagists and Virgils of small New Hampshire and Vermont farms. There came Amy Lowell, the youthful and splendid Edna St. Vincent Millay, S. Foster Damon, Robert Hillyer, Wilbert Snow, T. S. Eliot—until he put off his chicken-down and flew overseas and turned into a hawk and a vulture all at once—Charles Malam, John Holmes, and Frances Frost. And two men, the country suddenly discovered, in the teens of our century, had been writing a new kind of poetry all their own from the beginning of the period, and now, suddenly, they stood head and shoulders above all the others, not merely in New England, but in all America as well. The men were Edwin Arlington Robinson and Robert Frost. These last did not have to join a group and talk about poetry, or go on a revivalist's pilgrimage spreading a new gospel over the land. They had only to be themselves and write of life as they knew it and in the sober music that was in their own minds. That was revolution enough. It was a major revolution in the art of poetry. The kingdom coming and the day of jubilee for many people, slaves of life till now, rejected by art. For these two poets looked at life in a way that was very novel indeed for any poet in the world to look at it. They looked at it as men might rise up of a morning and stare at an entirely new sea after long months of storm, as a piece of beauty newly created and visited by a new light from clouds and sun. It is these two men whom I shall talk about in these lectures.

But before I do, I ought, I suppose, since I am a teacher of poetry, to say something about the older poetry, before I begin on this new. The older New England poetry bears, of course, certain strong family resemblances to the poetry of the South and to the older English poetry in general, and I shall be covering a remoter tradition in speaking of it. But it has, too, certain fundamental differences, and ones that are prophetic of our day. Some of these should be mentioned, as well. It is a glib and fashionable error of many modern critics to say that it has taken us two hundred years to get the lark out of American poetry. In the first place, we do have larks, and pretty fine ones, too. In the second place, that peculiarly English member of the family—one of the easiest and finest patterns of what a poet is, as Shelley has reminded us, and as I discovered for myself when I used to hear a score of English larks going up at once like so many silver bubbles through the thick sunshine of an English April afternoon on Shotover Hill, near Oxford—that bird, I say, was replaced in our literature by the American wild duck and the hermit thrush, from the eighteenth century on. These critics have to be reminded that Joel Barlow wrote of hasty pudding, albeit in Popeian couplets, that Longfellow wrote his two major poems on folklore of the New World, that Lowell wrote of New England courtings, and that one-half of all Whittier's songs and ballads are as American in subject matter as a tepee of Indian corn in the shock. The June Lowell describes so scientifically is an American June, not an English one. These men may have been American Scotts and Byrons, but they took their color from their native skies and trees. Whittier's *Snow-Bound* is at the opposite pole of the universe, in many ways, from Burns's *The Cotter's Saturday Night.* I don't refer merely to the grand canyons of Carrara marble of a Haverhill snowstorm outside the house, the like of which Scotland never knew. I mean the people inside. There is a barefoot boy beside the American hearth, but he is going to grow up into a man who will wear very fine shoes indeed. He is sitting among devout and homely people, like the people in Scotland, but they are also people whose lives are surrounded by rich books, rich opportunities for culture, for travel, for philosophy, for rising to the high seats of the world. The plain people of Burns are peasants; the plain folks of Whittier are Yankee princes. This local color, in setting and legends and nature, this spirit of ambition for betterment of bodies and minds, are native and New World materials in the poetry of the nineteenth century New England poets. They point ahead to the poetry of the present.

Yet, for all these new colors of American living, the most fundamental concepts of the older New England poets seem to us now traditionally English and definitely old-fashioned. If I had to put the essential quality in this old poetry into the fewest and plainest words—and that, I take it, is exactly the decorous and vital way to put essences today—I would say that the older poets were men who wore their best clothes all the time. They were orators. Not orators like the writer of the *Book of Ruth*, but orators like the *Book of Job*. They had a serious message to preach, and they preached it with the gestures that were second nature in the lives of our grandfathers. Behind all appearances was Truth, and Truth was a woman, and on a pedestal. And she had a face and a mind as high and severe over life as a Greek goddess. There is, to us now, something very feminine about the poetry of the nineteenth century. It is easy for us today to be gay-minded over all this. A man can laugh at his grandfather, though he never laughs at his father. But there is also something very single and comforting, something very wholesome and lovely about the poetic faith of our grandfathers. Their poetry was as naturally a part of their living as ours is now, and it is full of a calm that seems just now to be gone from the earth forever. "Study to be quiet." That precept—the word is as antiquated as Nineveh—of Izaak Walton came out of a time of bloodshed and civil war. Maybe, in spite of machines for rapid motion and communication, we may achieve such again. That these gestures of oratory in poetry were natural to Longfellow and Whittier, one can establish by recalling how even young children were taught to speak like orators from the cradle, with the appropriate gestures and intonations. Friday afternoon speaking was a foretaste of Sunday preaching. And the decorum of the old poetry shines through the samplers and the playthings of our grandparents' childhood. Even the multiplication table was dressed up and made as lovely as mathematics ever can be, in bright yarns and stitches. To be a poet was to be on a rostrum, head and shoulders above life. It was, except in very definite moments when levity was expected, to choose the best and put the best into the finest words in the language, the Sunday words, the library words, the parlor words. These were the words of life. Being a poet was to cultivate a high-souled attitude towards life, to have a goal ahead. *Excelsior*, to us, is a poem that seems almost like a caricature, or else something from the Aztecs. It was the staff of life to people who read it when the print was fresh. Lowly life the poet might often touch upon, but the village blacksmith became as eloquent a man as the man in the pulpit, and his devotion to work was linked with the whole pattern of a beneficent universe. Poems were psalms of life. The great and public, the great and private passions of all mankind, were the materials for the poets.

Romantic adventure, the hunger and thirst after things far distant from home, for the strange and the singular, be it mountains or buildings, or people or thoughts, were the life of poetry. Byron's romanticism runs like a thread through the lesser verses of nineteenth century New England. Almost all the minor poets were small Byrons. Love, a very wistful and unfleshly passion when at its best—and that was at all times—was a basic theme of the poets. It found itself an epic form at last, as it had found itself the allegorical one in the Middle Ages, in the Evangeline story, a major contribution to the poetry of the western hemisphere. How long ago all this was we can remind ourselves when we look at the very minor place romantic love holds in lyric poetry at the present. What was once a star of the first magnitude is now one of the fifth, and almost below the horizon. It is not that men no longer make love, but that our poets have lost their trust in the ancient spiritual concept of the centrality of a certain kind of love. Romantic love, fed by roots far back in the German forests and the Germanic sense of the worshipfulness of women as a strengthener of manhood, came into civilization in the Middle Ages. In France it became the courtly love, the spiritual nourisher of knighthood; divorced from economic and social responsibilities, it became, at its best, the wistful denial of life in the tale of the Celtic Tristram, and the resplendent energy, in the Italian Dante, that moves the sun and the other stars. The Renaissance domesticated that wild and aristocratic principle of life and made it a theme of all poets. And now, partly because we have explored scientifically the biological character of love, partly because we have lost our faith in most of the old patterns of centrality, romantic love has fallen to the level of the exploration of minor and private moods. Its complexity and intricate unity, which suited well with the Neo-Gothic architecture of our grandfathers' day, seems strangely archeological in this day of streamlined surfaces and bare mass.

The older poetry of New England wore its best clothes in style, as it wore them in its ideas. There was a definitely poetic vocabulary, there was the definitely poetic phrase. Poetry was a parlor art. And the parlors of our grandfolks, I need scarcely remind you, were, especially in New England, very serious parts of the house. The best rooms were both moral and intellectual retreats from the everyday world. They were consecrated to the highest moments of living and dying, the courtships and funerals. And the furnishings were in keeping. They were plush and silk and haircloth; they were prim and severe and uncommon. There was much of a loveliness that was preserved. The bouquets of everlasting roses there have much in common with the imagery of the older New England poets. The fancy of those poets, to us, seems often plush-like and stuffy. Nature was often the theme, but it seems a nature brought indoors, a nature at second hand. Elegance was a common word, then. It is the word that best explains the richness of the poetic style of that time.

Behind all this oratory and richness of mind was a now

rather outmoded doctrine of the improvement of life. This doctrine was especially strong in New England, thanks to our Puritan heritage. Each new generation, as it came along, was supposed to improve on the one that preceded it. Nor was this all. Each man's life was expected to enlarge as his years increased. Even the genial Holmes, the poet whose eyes twinkle most of all the eyes around Boston, has put the doctrine into words and into an imagery that came directly from that collection of polished jewels of the sea which was found on almost every New England parlor stand.

> Build thee more stately mansions, O my soul,
>   As the swift seasons roll!
>   Leave thy low-vaulted past!
> Let each new temple, nobler than the last,
> Shut thee from heaven with a dome more vast,
>   Till thou at length art free,
> Leaving thine outgrown shell by life's unresting sea!

As a boy, on the New England coast, I was as much moved by the sound of the pseudo-sea, in a parlor shell which I held to my ear, as I was by the actual sea that played its organs in the gales right at my doorstep.

In quoting this stanza from memory, I almost invariably change the adjective in the first line, and say *worthy*, instead of *stately*, and I omit the three exclamation points in my voice. I mention this because I think it is an important point. I—and I suspect other people do, too—subtract slightly but subtly from the oratorical magnificence of an older poet. I know I do not dare to put as much timbre into my voice as the readers of the past used to put into theirs.

According to this doctrine of the steady enlargement of man, my own poetry and the poetry of the two greatest modern New England poets I am going to talk about, ought to be more stately and magnificent in its rhythm, its imagery, and the wholeness of its belief in man's destiny, than that poetry which flourished in and around the Hub of the Universe sixty or seventy years ago. If people do turn in their graves, there must be some restlessness in those under the elms and the willows of Greater Boston.

This doctrine of improvement was a vital adjunct to Emerson's philosophy of the Superior Man. The breath in Bronson Alcott's ribs depended upon the enlargement of his horizon year by year. The Transcendentalists preached, not a philosophy of *being*, but a philosophy of *becoming*. Everything was growth. Everything was possible in the ordered unfolding of the years. The new man, and especially the new American man, had a constantly expanding universe in which to expand the vibrations of his soul. Nature should play her part. New lessons of harmony and nobility were to be learned there. The citizens of Brook Farm were to become finer husbandmen than the world had yet seen. Thoreau might be looking at wild life with new eyes, and setting down disturbing and uncomfortable things; but the best men knew that nature existed for the best purposes and could be made to improve with her masters. Even Whittier, a Quaker, a man of the religion of humility, who loved the plain people, was a reformer, a Crusader fired with zeal to enlarge humanity.

Behind these earnest men were great books of the past. Philosophy and science, the refinements of the noblest minds, the honey and gold of minds all the way from the secretaries of the Holy Ghost and Homer to the German philosophers of the nineteenth century. How could a world fail to progress when its intellectual treasures were a multiplication table, growing steadily and inevitably as the years grew? Behind most of the Boston poets were Harvard University, the Boston Latin School, a hundred new schools of improved pedagogy designed to make careless little boys and girls into masters of dialectic even before their trousers and skirts had reached the ground. Poets were men of letters and students of books as well as dreamers in the sun and lovers of living. Whitman, of course, for all his catholicity and love of manifestations of human nature that Boston could never approve, was touched by this same belief in the coming New World symphony in which the very lilacs and the seasons would be as much the teachers of wisdom as the older teachers, history and philosophy and religion. Hawthorne was ransacking the Old World, at the very time Goethe was declaring that America was more blessed by being free of ghosts, for all the old sins and ghosts Europe possessed, and bringing them over to help in the expansion of his moral universe by their colorful presence.

And behind all this western Atlantic culture, founded on the ideal of the constant betterment of men's minds and bodies, the western Atlantic was flowered with white

sails of ships and the plumes of the new steamboats, going and coming, bringing and taking the solid wares of
the world, on which the doctrine of the improvement of
mankind depended for its being and becoming. We are
apt to forget that fact—forget that the ocean was crowded
with life beside the Boston of 1850. Poets are apt to forget those ships going in and out of Newburyport, Portsmouth, Salem, Bath, Waldoboro, Boston, and the seaports
on the Connecticut coast. Poets are often near-sighted or
far-sighted persons. And the focus of their vision may
not take in the substantial matter that feeds their vision
of man's growth and improvement. The philosophy of
the Superior and Improving Man is a philosophy founded
on prosperity. The New England of 1850 was a New
England which was becoming another Phœnicia, another
England of the years when men borrowed the cobwebs of
May morning grass to wear at their throats and wrists,
when a son of a small-town leather merchant was writing
the best apology for kings and queens the world has ever
known. And in spite of the hiatus of the panic of 1857
and the Civil War, that prosperity continued until near
the beginning of our century.

The poetry of Longfellow and Emerson and Lowell
and Whittier was a poetry read in houses that were mansions. It was read in houses where back yards stretched
down around the curving world and took in the dreamlike mountains of Java and the fireflies of Borneo. Those
houses were full of furnishings from London and Paris
and Venice, from Canton and Ceylon. As a boy, I walked
on carpets woven in Brussels and heard stories that came

from under the Andes. And I was brought up in a farm-house. For even the small farmhouses of Maine, if they were on the coast, were mansions. They had colonnades and porticoes and fireplaces like the front elevation of the Parthenon, and they contained men of affairs as well as hoers of beans, men who had done great business in the waters of the wide world. There were uncles who recited chapters from the *Odyssey* between the sticks of firewood they were sawing for the kitchen cookstove. That New England of Longfellow was mostly a coast, where tall ships were a-making. Every farm that touched the water had its ship a year. Each child had his ship to set him up in the business of life. Housewives' names went around the Horn and into far waters on ships' sterns. Housewives went themselves, for that matter, and gave birth to their children in the lonely places of all the oceans. Cape Horn and Gibraltar came to be regular promontories of honeymoons.

The New England of the nineteenth century was a place where the living that got into poetry was a living of cultured men and women whose opportunities for action seemed limited only by the size of the world. It was the living that went on in big houses, or the small houses that were near enough to the big ones to have the best architecture and best books inside them. It was a land of economic good health. The American doctrine of un-limited opportunity for every mother's son was in its fullest bloom. Mills were humming like beehives along the Merrimac, the Androscoggin, and the Connecticut. They were filled with men whose eyes were blue and hair fair or brown, not the dark-haired of the shrunken mills of our own day. The small farms all the way north from Boston to the Canadian border were like beehives, too. The cellars and the attics were filled with the honey of summer labor, ears of popcorn, dried apples, jellies and jams, meal and flour and vegetables; and the large rooms between were filled with children, children enough to fill all the twelve rooms of the place. There were the hosts of farmers' sons who picked up the multitudinous stones, brought up anew by each spring plowing, and laid them up into the miles on miles of stonewalls which linked the loneliest communities into long chains of friendship. The farms were everywhere; they even climbed up the mountains, wherever oxen could climb, and spread tame fields and the sound of children's voices close to the deer and the hawks.

> Here further up the mountain slope
> Than there was ever any hope,
> My father built, enclosed a spring,
> Strung chains of wall round everything,
> Subdued the growth of earth to grass,
> And brought our various lives to pass.
> A dozen girls and boys we were.

But this is a modern New England poet writing this. That nineteenth century father did not know he had plowed a place too high for hope. Robert Frost knows what happened to that farm:

> The mountain seemed to like the stir,
> And made of us a little while—
> With always something in her smile.

Today she wouldn't know our name.
(No girl's, of course, has stayed the same.)
The mountain pushed us off her knees.
And now her lap is full of trees.

In our fathers' and grandfathers' days the wilderness blossomed, just as Scripture had said it should. The farmer was sure enough of himself and sure enough of his future to beget a big family. He had thousands of miles of comparatively undeveloped continent behind him. There were mills, and more coming. There were the roadways of the ocean to provide room for his seed. Better still, he had a supreme confidence in the rightness of his life and his neighbors', in the rightness of the patterns of his moral and religious beliefs. His homestead, if I may be allowed to describe it in my own verse,

was the sort
Men used to build when men could be
Alone in safety with their thoughts,
Their God, and their fecundity.

Not many of our modern houses are that safe. Or we do not think them so. Such a house had its own burying ground, next to the grape arbor. Men were that sure of the past and the future. Home burials were common. Robert Frost writes of one of them, but one in the lonesome latter years, when children are not so many, in one of his best poems, which he never reads in public. He has several such poems on thoughts that lie too deep for his spoken word.

Behind that older poetry of my people, that poetry of confidence, as I like to call it, was another populous edi-

fice. The white churches of New England were filled
with people, too. Even the small ones in the open fields
with spires the farmers ran their furrows by. I can remember one such at a crossroads where there were only five
houses within the bell's reach, where I went to hear ser-
mons as a boy in tight and Sunday shoes. The pews were
always full, as I remember them. I know ours was. The
congregation was made up of people who gave up a whole
day to going and coming in their best carriages. Life was
not too crowded for one whole day's being given up to
religion. Such a plain and solid fact lies behind the
poetry of *The Psalm of Life*, and *The Vision of Sir
Launfal*.

Underneath that poetry of confidence, there were designs of human belief that may often seem like the tenets
of Aztec religion to us now. These people—my people—
were surer than Chaucer was of his country, of his religion, and his literary patterns. They lived in a world
where vigor was increasing and the means of life ever
multiplying. It is small wonder they thought that improvement would be constant. They expected their particular world and their special prosperity to last. They
were sure of their ancestors. Ancestors, as we know now,
are the hardest things of all to be sure of. Till very lately
the Chinese were sure of theirs; but now even they are
beginning to lose faith, under the benefit of the bombs
of civilization. Being sure of one's forefathers is one of
the first fruits of prosperity. My people were sure of their
patterns of piety and filial and parental responsibility.
Psychology had not, as yet, uncovered the unhealthy, sun-

less things that may crawl under such solid stones. They believed in devotion to principles without the necessity of re-examining those principles three or four times a lifetime. Science had not yet completely investigated the beneficence in the universe out of existence. My people were sure of themselves. They were sure of the righteousness of life. That is different from believing in the rightness of life, as events have proved. Maybe belief in righteousness is easier. These people's economic and social foundations made it easy for them to keep the faith. They believed in the rightness of their erudition and their religion. Those two things went together to make up such a culture as they had. They believed in that culture. They were sure of the past. They were sure of the future.

They came rightly by a poetry of confidence. Poetry will reflect the nature of the era in which it exists. That is one of the surest propositions there are in this rather unstable world. It is surer than many laws of physics and bills of rights. Not that poets are reporters and propagandists. The best of them never are. Robinson and Frost are not. But poets do present the eternal and the changeless in the designs of the times, in the special doctrines and moral patterns and in the vocabulary native to their day. Confidence will have its poetry of confidence. Doubt will have its poetry of doubt. Poetry can survive under both banners. For it is an ageless thing. It is a defier of time and a defier of the accidents, whether of prosperity or want. The poetry of confidence had its right world to flourish in.

How is it now with that New England where it flourished?

For the answer, I should like to take you up along the Kennebec. That is the river which flows through the heart of Maine. That is the river Edwin Arlington Robinson grew up on. It was along a Kennebec river road that he walked as a boy, one hot afternoon, near the end of summer, to be with his friends, Isaac and Archibald, two old men. These two men were near their end. Each lived alone in a big house built for a man's host of children. There are many such big houses left along the Kennebec River. And mostly they are places kept by one old man or one old woman. Many of these are not so sure of their sunset world as Isaac and Archibald were. Many of their houses are not so well painted or in so good repair. The fields around them are smaller fields. Year by year, the balsams, the wild trees that the farmers pushed into the gullies and up to the hilltops, have taken strength and are marching back, taking back the land of their ancestors. The wild is coming back. You may come upon porticoed houses falling into ruins in the perpetual shade of enveloping trees that have grown from their very floors. There are fewer farms than there were fifty years ago. There is more wild land in Maine than there was one hundred years ago. This is a tragic thing for old eyes to see. This is a tragedy to men whose bodies are too old and spent to fight the fight over that their forefathers won from the forest. Familiar old landmarks, covered over slowly, year by year. A roadway lost. Another light gone out for good in the house across the valley. The nights

3

growing more enormous, with fewer lighted windows. Whippoorwills singing nearer the house each spring. Stone-walls are lost among the maples. A deer comes upon tame apple trees in a small clearing in the very heart of his forests; the animal stands and stares, but fear leaves him, and he comes closer and falls to nibbling at the golden carpet under the tree which the frost has spread out in one night, the deer eats the apples some man designed for his grandchildren. But the man is under the earth now, and his grandchildren are in a distant place or have never come to being. A man can come upon a graveyard in the thick woods. The headstones are slanted, and some have fallen under the powerful twisting of live hemlock roots. An old man stirs uneasily in his bed in a house too big for one old man.

Out on the river where a dozen ships used to come up under full sail every day after the spring ice was out, there is nothing moving at all. Not even a steamer goes by. The great shipyards that once swarmed with young men are gone as completely as towns of the Indians. The great icehouses have sunk into the earth. There are wharves and warehouses rotting away in Gardiner and Hallowell, Bowdoinham, Richmond, and Bath. This is the landscape that looms in the sad and dreamlit pages of *Amaranth*. This is the decaying world the artist Fargo wandered through, a world of silence and despair,

> Never a silence like this now
> On ships and wharves and water could have been
> Since moving time began. He had come back
> Once more to a lost world where all was gone

But ghostly shapes that had no life in them,
And to the wrong world he would once have left
By the wrong door.

Robinson must have walked often by the rotting piles of
the port of Tilbury Town, to have them come back so in
such dreams. And the sea out beyond the Kennebec's
mouth is empty of ships now also. The coast that once
was the cradle of captains is empty today. I think I wrote
a brief history of Maine as the subtitle of my book *Kennebec*; I wrote it in these words, *Cradle of Americans*.
There is no such eloquent a piece of furniture as a cradle,
and an empty one is all the more so. This is the history
of my state: Maine has always bred her best children for
other states farther west. Empty cradles are everywhere
in Maine; in towns, in houses, in minds. And the saddest
of all are those in minds. So the story runs, now, down
the whole New England coast. And Portsmouth and
Newburyport, Salem and the ports of Connecticut, have
their empty waterfronts.

So it goes, too, with the farms all over northern New
England. The White Mountains and the Green have
grown back into their ancient extent. They have pushed
the farms off their knees and taken back their green and
ancient children. Frost knows the tragedy of tame land
going back to the wild. He writes often of coming upon
houses lost in the mountains. We hear him talking to
himself, as lonely New Englanders often do, in *The
Census-Taker*:

No lamp was lit. Nothing was on the table.
The stove was cold—the stove was off the chimney—

And down by one side where it lacked a leg.
The people that had loudly passed the door
Were people to the ear but not the eye.
They were not on the table with their elbows.
They were not sleeping in the shelves of bunks.
I saw no men there and no bones of men there.
I armed myself against such bones as might be
With the pitch-blackened stub of an axe-handle
I picked up off the straw-dust covered floor.
Not bones, but the ill-fitted window rattled.
The door was still because I held it shut
While I thought what to do that could be done—
About the house—about the people not there.
This house in one year fallen to decay
Filled me with no less sorrow than the houses
Fallen to ruin in ten thousand years
Where Asia wedges Africa from Europe.
Nothing was left to do that I could see
Unless to find that there was no one there
And declare to the cliffs too far for echo,
"The place is desert and let whoso lurks
In silence, if in this he is aggrieved,
Break silence now or be forever silent.
Let him say why it should not be declared so."
The melancholy of having to count souls
Where they grow fewer and fewer every year
Is extreme where they shrink to none at all.
It must be I want life to go on living.

This talking of a new poet has a strange flatness in it
and a haunting, virile sincerity, too, after the finer rhythms
and finer phrases of the sorrows of the earlier New England poets. Frost can laugh, too, at the spectacle of man's
inability to people the wilderness. Laughter is often this

poet's salvation. So he explains the name of Still Corners
in his poem *New Hampshire*—the name comes, not from
silence or whiskey, but from the fact the place is still
just a crossroads, still corners in the woods.

In these northern farmlands that are becoming forests,
where houses grow fewer year by year, strange changes
come over the people that have stayed. *Staying* is the
word Frost uses for it, not *living*. A woman listens to
the branch of a pine tree against her window, a wild
branch that has no business to be there where a tame
branch should be. It is more than a symbol; the fears of
Frost's people are more than such conventional things.
This is a thing that can get inside a brain and grow:

> She had no saying dark enough
>   For the dark pine that kept
> Forever trying the window-latch
>   Of the room where they slept.
>
> The tireless but ineffectual hands
>   With every futile pass
> Made the great tree seem as a little bird
>   Before the mystery of glass!
>
> It never had been inside the room,
>   And only one of the two
> Was afraid in an oft-repeated dream
>   Of what the tree might do.

People living in this new northern New England loneliness may fall to odd rituals of behavior.

> Always—I tell you this they learned—
> Always at night when they returned
> To the lonely house from far away

To lamps unlighted and fire gone gray,
They learned to rattle the lock and key
To give whatever might chance to be
Warning and time to be off in flight:
And preferring the out- to the in-door night,
They learned to leave the house-door wide
Until they had lit the lamp inside.

Sometimes a man has no time left for anything else but keeping the wildness and the loneliness at bay:

The house was black as winds could dye it
   And lonelier because wild bees
Were in its eaves. The Queen Anne doorway
   Was choked up with wildcherry trees.

At the twilight little owls
   Cried in the trees companionless
And made it seem a thousand miles
   To the nearest happiness.

The owner of the house was strong,
   But he was only one alone
Against a thousand subtle roots
   Creeping where his seeds were sown.

This master of a house besieged
   Had no time to choose a wife
Or make friends for himself, for he
   Fought for more than merely life.

The forest had half won its fight
   To win the buildings back for good,
There were other things at work
   Than the death-ticks in the wood.

The man would often catch himself
   Listening when he came from chores,

And he had grown to be adept
  At taking time to open doors.

For his ways he gained the title
  Of queer; none seemed to understand
That he was one who stood in darkness
  Shielding a candle with his hand.

That is how I have tried to describe one kind of New England tragedy.

It is a strangely changed New England from the one Whittier knew when he walked the Crystal Hills of New Hampshire looking for bright legends of the Sokokis. It is sometimes lonelier than when the Indians held it. A place where much living has been and is no longer there is lonelier than a virgin wilderness. And to the south in the great cities that machinery has built greater, in a Boston larger than Emerson's, there is something very vital gone. Here are empty cradles, too. But here it is not people so much as a pattern that is wanting. Confidence has gone out of men, confidence in certain designs of the spirit that were once the breath of life to New Englanders, from Transcendentalists to men in the street who basked in their optimism.

But it is a blind man and a lost man who believes that poetry may not outlive a material and spiritual prosperity of one particular kind. When certain patterns of confidence are destroyed, men discover new ones. That is the history of the human race, and that has been the history of poetry, which has played the part of man's great healer from the times before history began. Other charters of the ancient rights to belief there are. The poets will find them, and they will fit them to a music that men of their day will listen to. If the music is to be plainer, it will be so. If the creeds are to be less exact and sure, they will be wider and more courageous, perhaps.

So, as we shall see, our new poets of New England have found new music and a new matter for a very ancient art.

THE ARTIST IN THE WRONG WORLD

This afternoon, because of the nature of the two poets with whom I am dealing and because of the plan I have set myself to follow, I shall speak mostly about the work of Edwin Arlington Robinson. But I shall begin this paper on *The Artist in the Wrong World* with a rather long quotation from the poems of Robert Frost, and I shall have an occasion to return to the happier of these two great New England poets at the end.

Happiness is an old-fashioned term, and perhaps I ought not to use that word, now that I have finished with the past and have come into the midst of my subject and the modern world. But even if the word is an old one and seems rather naïve in the face of so much modern psychology, I think it still has a very definite meaning for people. When I describe Frost as a happier poet than Robinson, I think most people will agree with me that there is a legitimate distinction to be made between these men and that some such term will do to describe it. Robert Frost has found, in spite of troubles greater than most men are called on to face—and there is a new instance of trouble just as I say this—more things in life to feel well about, and even feel sure about, than has Edwin Arlington Robinson. Feeling well and sure about life may still be called happiness, I suppose. Robinson had his troubles, too. He was a poet for many years, as was Frost, before he found a wide circle of readers. He saw hard times. He lived to see better. But in better times or worse, his genius moved on lonelier levels than Frost's has moved. He was always more alone. The people who knew him best of all speak of his aloneness. He was as incapable of forming friendships widely as Frost is incapable of avoiding such. And Robinson found more of his eloquence in men's failures. Eloquence can be found in failure just as surely as in success. Wisdom can show itself in finding the flaws in the world. But doubt and negation are unhappy things. And great though they may be in the music of a magnificent and brave mind, they are less magnificent than the answers the poet can discover to the questions life poses. Robinson found some sure answers. But they shall be my matter in later papers. Today I shall be more concerned with the unanswered questions in his poems. Yet if there is more of disintegration than integration in my study today, I beg you to remember that disintegrations can have their creative power, or else Sophocles and Shakespeare have written in vain.

And now for my quotation from Frost. It comes from the poem, *A Fountain, a Bottle, a Donkey's Ears and Some Books*, in the volume *New Hampshire*. You may recall the situation in the poem. The narrator has been exploring one of the empty cradles of a New Hampshire mountain township. He and his guide, Davis, had set out to find a baptismal font of the early Mormons. But they had lost their way and had brought up at a deserted house which Davis recognized, at the mountain's foot. They decided to enter.

"Excuse me if I ask you in a window
   That happens to be broken," Davis said.
The outside doors as yet have held against us.
I want to introduce you to the people
Who used to live here.   They were Robinsons.
You must have heard of Clara Robinson,
The poetess who wrote the book of verses
And had it published. It was all about
The posies on her inner window sill,
And the birds on her outer window sill,
And how she tended both, or had them tended:
She never tended anything herself.
She was 'shut in' for life. She lived her whole
Life long in bed, and wrote her things in bed.
I'll show you how she had her sills extended
To entertain the birds and hold the flowers.
Our business first's up attic with her books."

We trod uncomfortably on crunching glass
Through a house stripped of everything
Except, it seemed, the poetess's poems.
Books, I should say!—if books are what is needed.
A whole edition in a packing-case,
That, overflowing like a horn of plenty,
Or like the poetess's heart of love,
Had spilled them near the window toward the light,
Where driven rain had wet and swollen them.
Enough to stock a village library—
Unfortunately all of one kind, though.
They had been brought home from some publisher
And taken thus into the family.
Boys and bad hunters had known what to do
With stone and lead to unprotected glass:
Shatter it inward on the unswept floors.
How had the tender verse escaped their outrage?

By being invisible for what it was,
Or else by some remoteness that defied them
To find out what to do to hurt a poem.
Yet oh! the tempting flatness of a book,
To send it sailing out the attic window
Till it caught wind, and, opening out its covers,
Tried to improve on sailing like a tile
By flying like a bird (silent in flight,
But all the burden of its body song),
Only to tumble like a stricken bird,
And lie in stones and bushes unretrieved.
Books were not thrown irreverently about.
They simply lay where some one now and then,
Having tried one, had dropped it at his feet
And left it lying where it fell rejected.
Here were all those the poetess's life
Had been too short to sell or give away.

Here, in this description of an attic full of poetry books lost in the heart of a new forest, there is, for me, a kind of double symbolism. These books here are a small elegy of a whole world, a whole body of poetry. A kind of poetry that seems *shut in* to us now. It is a poetry that was once a part of life. But the nature in it was a tended nature, a nature brought indoors and often identified with a moral. It is poetry *inside*, from in bed, poetry at two removes from life. And here it lies now, neglected, in a place where the only inhabitants are trees! As if the trees had come in to set the nature captive in the pages of this poetry book free once more. That poetry had been a sort of patent of nobility which all the best New England people aspired to. It was definitely felt, even at its weakest, to be art. We do not feel that our poorer poetry today is art. That is one difference between our times and the older. That poetry was an illumination of that world which the heroes and heroines—if you will forgive another old-fashioned word for worthy people!—of Edwin Arlington Robinson have sometimes tried in vain to find their way back to. Here it lies lapped only in green and vegetative life.

And, for the other symbol here, there is, in this poem of Frost's, some indication of Frost's way of escape, by humor and by human nature, not only from the tragic connotations of this situation, but from the ruins of that older New England into very present and very pulsing New England life.

The new New England is a place that is hard on poets, as on all artists. Certainly, it is harder on the smaller ones than the old one was. And, of course, it resembles the rest of the earth today in this respect of being hard on its artists. Perhaps, in the long run, all times and places are hard on poets. Perhaps we would never have poets worth their salt, if this were not so. But I think that times of great change are harder than times of stability. And the present is a time of great change.

Edwin Arlington Robinson is the poet of these hard times. Being a major poet, he writes, of course, of a wider country than the small cluster of New England states. Most of his longer poems are set far back in distant times and places, or they are acted out in a peculiarly generalized locality where particular landmarks are hard to identify. His geography is a geography of a gray place, and the trees and houses often have no particular individuality or style of leaf or architecture. His trees are trees, as Frost's are maples and pines. Yet, all the same, Robinson's thinking, it seems to me, is peculiarly a New Englander's, and his characters, though often as faceless as dreams, are New Englanders in their brains and their hearts. Never so local a set of people in all poetry, I think. His people may be queens and princes, but they are also friends of mine who live in a particular kind of house in Maine and New Hampshire. Many of Robinson's characters, the earliest ones and the latest, feel that they are artists living in a wrong world. These words, which I have taken for the title of my lecture today, are Robinson's own. They come from that late poem which I think is one of his most characteristic and most revealing, *Amaranth*, a poem I shall use often as an illustration.

This wrong world which the artists Fargo and Atlas find themselves in can easily be called the new New England, for Fargo surely is a New Englander. Atlas, you will recall, is a stevedore turned artist, and Fargo, before he made his journey into a dreamlike region where Amaranth taught him the virtue of seeing things as they are, had left off being a mediocre painter to become a first-class maker of pumps.

These people, Amaranth and Fargo, are my friends, I say. And I know what houses to look in to find them at home. They are the Big-House New Englanders. They are found in the greatest number along a strip, say, a day's ride by a carriage in width, along the whole New England seashore or navigable river valleys. As we have many rivers, that means quite a fair part of New England.

These men are the sons of families who once had everything, from ships and money to minds that were sure they had an important part to play in the world; sons of families dispossessed both of material and spiritual wealth. Loss of material wealth hurts a good deal. The loss of spiritual wealth hurts a great deal more. These are sons of rulers, and they no longer rule. They are not at home among the almost intelligent machines that carry people and feed people and make them as comfortable as prize stock on a model dairy farm. I know what these people have to suffer and think about, because I have spent evenings with them, and some of them have my blood in them. They are very interesting people to spend evenings with. They do not have so much to say as Robinson has them say, but they think what he puts into their minds. Their silences can be very eloquent. They have very fine things to look at in the way of mantels and porticoes and cupolas and rows of elms, but such fine things can be very hard to live with if one has nothing fine to do in the world. The people can sell their big houses to the new summer people. Some of them have to do that. But even such a step will not take them into the midst of life. The money they receive from the sale will be as vain a thing as the beauty and white clapboards and green blinds which they inherited from their fathers. For they are no longer directors of living. They are fewer than they were in Robinson's boyhood. They see their numbers decreasing steadily year by year, even in Maine, where things are longer at lasting. They see their unmarried children growing gray. They see some of their number retreating into their houses and into longer and longer silences inside those houses, and it is like doors being closed on themselves. They see some of their kin turning eccentric and queer. That is the hardest of all to bear. They still cling, many of them, to the big houses, but they know themselves for what they are. They are the dispossessed. Their houses are like very fine tombs. It is not the lack of warmth, either, in rooms where fireplaces no longer burn through the long winters. It is a warmth that has gone out in themselves.

Big-House people, did I say? Let me remind you that my adjective *big* stands for something more important than size. Some of the best Big-House people live in places that would be called cottages outside New England. But even these small places have, generally, fine architecture and, what is more, they once had ceilings that went up to the stars and took in the constellations there as their back yards once took in Java Head and Cape Horn. It is only lately, since 1880 or thereabouts, that the ceilings have come down so low that the people who live there have to go with their heads bowed. All these houses, these twelve-roomed ones and the five-roomed, once housed princes of a sort. They housed fine books of the past that were still thumbed and free of dust, that gave new strength to the ideas of the men who lived there and had their hands in fine white pine and China tea, in laws and moral issues. Even the very small boys had their great companions, Lancelot and Tristram and Arthur and Achilles were as real to these small boys as their older brothers. It was such a boy that walked out along the

Kennebec river road with one old man to visit another one in a long ago summer. And his head, as those of you who remember your *Isaac and Archibald*, one of the greatest poems this century or any has produced, was full of those great old gentlemen, and he kept thinking of them while he basked in the gentleness and gentility of these two old Kennebec men, his friends.

These are the people whom, before they have cooled into history, Robinson has given to the world as citizens with a tragic intensity to them that will insure their living for a long time to come.

I should like to say something about the code of these Big-House New Englanders. For their begetters had worked out a very fine code for them. It is fine, even though it has not much place in the world nowadays, and depended too much on a set of circumstances and prosperity that were bound not to last. I suppose it is a thing to make me suspect, to use the word *aristocrat*, in these days when it may be confused with Tory or Bourbon. But I come from a Republican state, and I have Republican notions of what an aristocrat should be. If that is a paradox, I hope I may be forgiven it. Hard times make queer bedfellows of us all! The Big-House people were aristocrats, both in their ideas about the means to life and the purpose of it. They were all the stronger aristocrats because they were descended, like some of the First Families of Virginia, from middle-class Englishmen. The strongest aristocracies are built out of middle classes. That is why revolutions now are so hard on the middle-class people. Revolutionists know where the life they

4

strike at lies most alive. The Big-House people took the means to life for granted. They had the books and the fine furniture and the racial oneness necessary as foundations to aristocracy. They had them, and they forgot them, which is still a definition of gentility as it was in the Middle Ages. They did not think about their cut-glass. It was the outsider, the man from the small New England house, the country cousin, who thought about what Robert Frost, in Small-House glee, calls a "cut-glass dinner in Boston." Frost met a lovely woman at such a dinner, a witch "new style," as he calls her:

> Her husband was worth millions.
> I think he owned some shares in Harvard College.

Frost, as we shall see, believes that some crudity is necessary as salt to a poet's good health.

But the Big-House people had other more distinguishing qualities. And these they were very conscious of, maybe too much for their own ultimate survival. Charity was a part of their code. The best of them could pardon the breaking of laws much older than their own:

> There was a woman in our town
> On whom the fashion was to frown;
> But while our talk renewed the tinge
> Of a long-faded scarlet fringe,
> The man Flammonde saw none of that,
> And what he saw we wondered at—
> That none of us, in her distress,
> Could hide or find our littleness.

The man Flammonde also saw promise in a Maine boy and helped him become a famous scholar. The man Flam-

monde came from outside Tilbury Town, which is high
Gardiner on the Kennebec River, and he had a foreign
air. But it is easy to see in him a rather full delineation
of the Big-House code of New England, and I like to
think he must have come from some New England place.
Reticence is another quality which these people possessed
and which their sons still possess. There are shadows and
sorrows in Maine. It could not be otherwise in a place
where culture has been a long time and where now the
economic foundations of that culture have long since
crumbled away. But Robinson's people do not speak
much of their grief. They think about it, but keep it to
themselves. It has never been the habit in Maine and
other northern New England places for a man to roll up
his shirt and show his scars to the world. Courage is
another of the code's parts. It goes along with reticence
often. It keeps a man alive, and it sends him home like
Richard Cory, a Big-House gentleman who kept up appearances, to put a bullet through his head. The code con-
tains the peculiar northern kind of tenderness, too, that
shows oftenest in people like Aunt Imogen who could, in
all justice, be loving to her nephews where a mother could
only afford to be fair. The code had loyalty to the past
and to tradition, of course. Ambition used to be a part
of the code, and the desire to improve one's mind and
manor; but that was in the old days. But, above all, the
code had as its absolute and unvarying requirement a
sense of one's sufficiency and righteousness. I had almost
said rightness, for that old New England sufficiency had
most of the characteristics of an extreme sense of right-

ness. The Puritans who sired many of the Big-House people saw to that. I had an aunt, and I suppose all New Englanders have had an aunt like her, who never allowed my doubts of the rightness of her authority to check her in her inculcation of principles. She was granite and juniper and sharp evergreens that present daggers to the outside world. Morality and beauty were the same things to her. As I have exclaimed in an essay about her, what an aunt to found a universe!

Yet Flammonde accomplished very little, Richard Cory was a failure, and King Cole and Theophilus and many others came to no good. How is it that the Big-House people do not work out their destiny and accomplish the fine purposes implicit in their code? It is for the simple reason that the world which created the big house has fallen into decay and left the Big-House people without any life to shape to the code. Three as simple things as the disintegration of an economic fabric, the coming of a new kind of knowledge, and the insufficiency of the code itself have accounted for the presence of fine minds in a world that has no place for them. For the first, the leadership of New England in sea trade and manufactures passed westward and southward, to other places, or vanished into thin air. The old English stock has been replaced as producers of economic wealth by labor by newer European stocks. More important than that, a new kind of knowledge, a new evaluation of the physical world, which is science, of course, has come in everywhere. Science might be termed a search for a sort of indiscriminate truth, that is, a truth that is no respecter of persons or codes of gentility. It often aims, not at choosing the best so much as examining all. It tends to level distinctions whether in clothes we wear or ideas we entertain. It is the ally of the lowliest—though it may prove a Judas to them—and sometimes of the lowest breeds of men. It may substitute number for quality. It has become able, by combining chemistry with astronomy, to miscount whole new universes of stars. It can even tell vast and important untruths about Troy and Helen and mankind in general and the solar system. It is always hard on the aristocrats, no matter who they may be, as it is notoriously hard on the gods and artists. It may be especially destructive of poets. Worst of all, there was an insufficiency in the old New England Big-House code. It was not founded upon standards that are wide enough for a whole world to grow by.

It is one kind of poem to see what happens to a seashell after the tide has ebbed, or after it has been left on the land in unaccustomed sunlight. Any New England pasture ledge—and New England pastures are mostly ledges—are such poems. You can see a new and strange kind of loveliness which the mussel or cockle or crab never knew it possessed in the sea, brought out clearly. Delicate azure lines, jewel-like excrescences. The spines fall from the sea-urchin and leave a crust of jewels where they stood. The shells are more fragile. But they are not the shells they were in the ocean. A touch will powder them to dust. Those shells are like the people E. A. writes about. Lovely human designs, but stranded in a cruelly hostile place, lost and wasted on the world. Their symmetries stand out more sharply, but they are closer to annihilation, and ready to fall at the touch of doom. All that is left of the novelist Amelia Watchman, when she looks Amaranth, the teller of truth, in the eyes, is a little sprinkle of dust between the pages of a book.

That makes me think of those books I began with today, the books of poems by Clara Robinson, which we left behind there in that rotting house the trees had closed in on, in that lost New Hampshire place. "Driven rain had wet and swollen them," you remember. These were fine things—at least they were finely built books—going back to nothing. These books could not stand the test of time and the old seasons. Seasons are harder on books even than on men's hands and minds. Being a poet, I like to play at the game of "understood relations." Is it accidental that there should happen to be in the universe a New Hampshire poet Robinson? I knew still another Robinson, and she was another poet, too, and one near the banks of the Kennebec. She wrote old-fashioned poetry also. She never discovered, any more than did Clara Robinson who left a trunkful of her one book, that she was a poet in the wrong world. That is at least one difference between her and Edwin Arlington Robinson.

If you wish to know what happens to people in big houses when their fortunes and philosophies ebb away, go and live in any small New England place. The people are there, though they may not all have the ironical names Robinson gives them. They have some that are ironical enough, though. For the older New England ran to Old Testament names that are right ones for heads of clans

and givers of laws. These people have no laws to give
now and no clans to head. They go about looking for the
old sure absolutes that made their fathers successful and
happy men, and they find that absolutes are not the
fashion now. Most of them are along in years, especially
since the time E. A. was a boy in Tilbury. They live
rather lonely existences, though some of them are restless and move about. They go like automatons, like John
Evereldown, who walks the dark road to Tilbury Town
and women, though he is a weary old man and desire is
a curse upon him:

> " I follow the women wherever they call,—
>   That's why I'm going to Tilbury Town.
> God knows if I pray to be done with it all,
>   But God is no friend to John Evereldown.
> So the clouds may come and the rain may fall,
> The shadows may creep and the dead men crawl,—
> But I follow the women wherever they call,
>   And that's why I'm going to Tilbury Town."

Some of them stand on rotting wharves and look down
at evil, dead waters where ships do not ride any more.
The water fascinates them, and they cannot take their
eyes away, and they think of the end of things. Voices
often call them from the grave, as they call Luke Havergal
and tell him the one way to peace. The old qualities of
mind that used to keep New England people sweet in
their strength have often turned sour in the children, like
the famous New England conscience:

> And Conscience always has the rocking-chair,
> Cheerful as when she tortured into fits
> The first cat that was ever killed by Care.

The children sacrifice themselves for their elders; aunts, for their nephews. They make a cult of care. Their friends may grow to be like King Jasper's friend Hebron, an old man of the sea who clings to one's back and weights life down like a nightmare. These people become eccentrics as the years go by emptier and emptier. Brothers may fall silent and never speak to each other in the same house. The devotion of sisters may turn into hate. The houses are too big for people growing small. I have tried to describe such people:

> They lived together in a house
>   Too big for women growing old;
> One after one, they closed the doors
>   On rooms surrendered to the cold.
>
> They had too many things to keep
>   Against the stealthy moth and sun,
> Too many keepsakes to protect
>   Ever to think of using one.
>
> Their lives contracted till at last
>   Their orbit was the kitchen fire;
> They sat to think where they had cooked,
>   Empty of comment and desire.
>
> Keen ways they learned to keep their souls
>   From filling one another's need;
> They found each other's tender spots
>   And knew best how to make them bleed.
>
> The sparrows and the robins made
>   Their love each year around their gate;
> Inside the house two women aged
>   And sat together in their hate.

Heaven lit the appletrees
  Beyond the curbing of their well;
Inside four walls, in one small room,
  There was room enough for hell.

Yet there was something holy, too,
  In their fine art of giving pain;
They moved like ancient tragedy,
  Single as martyrs in old Spain.

In these years of aimlessness,
  Among our lives without design,
It was as if there yet survived
  A god to offer poisoned wine.

Such people grow to like their loneliness. That is a bad sign. They grow to love it. And that is a worse one. They rebuild the world to ideas that grow in silence. They grow shy of men. They look down when they talk to those they meet:

"Stafford was a likely man with ideas of his
    own—
Though I could never like the kind that likes
    to live alone;
And when you met, you found his eyes were
    always on your shoes,
As if they did the talking when he asked you
    for the news."

It is not a good thing to have people who look up only when they are alone. And from eccentricity, it is but a short step to things that are done in the night, final things that show how thin the walls are between us and the Middle Ages, between men and strange presences which science does not believe in but which can be as real as flames in the night to men who find themselves trapped in the wrong world, with vast ideas they must keep to themselves:

> "An apple tree that's yet alive saw something,
>   I suppose,
> Of what it was that happened there, and what
>   no mortal knows,
> Some one on the mountain heard far off a
>   master shriek,
> And then there was a light that showed the
>   way for men to seek.
>
> "We found it in the morning with an iron bar
>   behind,
> And there were chains around it; but no
>   search could ever find,
> Either in the ashes that were left, or anywhere,
> A sign to tell of who or what had been with
>   Stafford there."

Evil can come in upon lonely people, people who live too much by themselves, too much to themselves. Straight old-fashioned evil, maybe in a godlike form, but with a face twisted awry and lit by an upward-shining light instead of the light of the morning star whose name the godlike form once wore.

Such are the lost and lonely people of Edwin Arlington Robinson. These are the shells that change of times has thrown out of their element, to bleach out into the ghostly patterns of wasted if beautiful designs. These are the tragedies E. A. saw around him as a boy in Gardiner. Small designs of sorrow and sadness, you may say, but they would grow to become the patterns behind all sensitive living as time went on. They would grow with the boy and become universal patterns in all he saw as a man. They would become the houseful of thwarted artists in *Amaranth* and the thwarted family in *King Jasper*. These New England tragedies account, it seems to me, for a great deal of this poet's peculiar makeup. These small tragedies which a man might easily miss who was unfamiliar with the life that goes on so quietly and lonely behind the blinds of New England cast a shadow over E. A. in his boyhood, and it was a shadow he could never walk out of even when he walked, lonely, as he was always to be, with the crowds of New York City and in the sunshine of that small utopian place, a modest, right world for artists at last, the MacDowell Colony of Peterboro, New Hampshire, which meant so much to him in his later years. It is this shadow, I believe, that made Robinson what Robert Frost called him in a letter he wrote me a week or so ago, a man "cast in the mold of sadness."

When I think of such tragedies in the little towns and on the lonely farms of the place I know best of all on this earth, I often wonder what it is in Maine, and in other regions north of Boston and even to the west and south of it in New England, that makes the process of human disintegration so swift and so complete. I know New England is an old place, where people have been for a long time. Such places are the ones where a man can look for tragedy. People become in-bred, blood runs thin, the economic foundations crumble, people peter out and grow eccentric and queer. But I know other much older places where people have lived for scores of generations, where they have intermarried, suffered reversals of fortune; and yet no such disintegrations are to be found there. Old England, for an example. I have lived in a village there eight hundred years old. I came to know everybody in the place. There were troubles and eccentricities, and even sin. But there was nowhere there the saddening spectacle of people creeping away and shutting themselves up in their houses, growing queer. There were none of those sudden and complete annihilations in families I had known in my own Maine town. People did not stop having big families and big ideas, they did not creep away defeated and shut themselves up from life. And during that very time I was living in England, a woman I had known as a boy, who had turned her back on life in my town, had turned her back on the community first, on her friends next, and finally on her church—that was the last thing to go—and had lived without going out of her house for seven years, was found starved and frozen in her bed. She was found dead in a house full of fine furniture, some pieces of which, if she had sold them, would have brought money enough to keep her in comfort the rest of her days.

I have tried to account for such a difference. Is it something in the sharp American air that causes such disintegration? Something in our weather? Our stock is largely the same as in those little English towns. Why does it deteriorate here and not there? Maybe it is because we lack two places of good health the English have kept

from ancient days, the inn and the church. The inn we
have never had, in New England. Our church once meant
much to all the community all the days of the week. Now
it means only an hour of a Sunday, to many. The church
of Old England has survived many changes. The New
England church is a place growing empty like the large
houses that once sent their cohorts of children and men
and women out into the midst of life. I know many country churches whose blinds have been closed for many
years, whose only congregations are the sharp wasps.
Churches, I know, are not religion, but empty ones are a
sign of decay in something that our grandparents knew as
religion. Maybe the old New England religion, like the
old New England code, was lacking in power to last. Or
maybe it was too hard a thing always to live up to. There
have been many such too hard and too fine things that
have had to go. Many in ancient times, many in the Middle Ages, and many now. Robinson's people are not
people who go to church.

Robinson's way of escape from despair in his world,
that is the wrong one for the artist, is his own peculiar
irony. It is the way of Fargo and Amaranth. Courage to
face disaster is a bitter flower, but it is "the flower that
never fades." Robinson can see life through because he
can see through life. In his poem *Amaranth*, the artists
have only an audience of artists themselves. Too many
of our poets today have only audiences of poets. That is
a sign of danger. That is why they write as they do, with
a sense of weariness and futility. But nearly all the
characters in *Amaranth* have the ability to laugh at them-

selves. *That*, unfortunately, cannot be said of many of
our modern poets. Not all our wearier present-day poets
have that power. Atlas laughs at his own futuristic paint-
ing. Evensong, the poet, laughs at his own verses. Even
Ampersand, the cat, can see through felinity and explain
it in the terms of the mechanistic philosophy. It is some
kind of salvation to know how beautifully articulated a
wrong world can be and how well it works:

> "I don't like it,"
> Said Ampersand—who promptly caught a fly
> And anxiously chewed air until he found it.
> "Excuse me. He was flying to his fate,
> And here was I, ordained to swallow him.
> You call it nature's law. I, being a cat,
> Call it a problematical free will.
> If there's a difference, no philosophers,
> I'm told, have caught it yet. No, I don't like it—
> I mean the picture. And if you have eyes
> That are not liars, you are not proud of it
> Along your back. There are no crinkles in it.
> Why do you do it? You were here before,
> I am informed; and why are you here now?
> You must know where you are. Miss Watchman knew,
> Although she never said it—not even to me.
> And there was not much that I didn't know
> About Miss Watchman. She told everything
> To me—except that she knew where she was.
> But she liked writing more than she liked truth,
> Or life, and I'm not saying that she was foolish,
> Or self-destroyed, in doing what she liked best.
> When I can seize the possibility
> Of doing what I like best, I always do it;
> And I have no devouring aspirations

Consuming me with unacknowledged lies.
The more I learn of men's and women's folly
In trying to make their wishes their belief,
The more I'm rather content to be a cat;
And cats, you may have guessed, are not without
Their ingrained and especial vanities,
For which there is no cure. Nature in us
Is more intractable and peremptory;
Wherefore you call us feral and ferocious,
Which is unfair to us; for the same God
Who sees a sparrow on the ground shows us
The way to catch him, and we cannot choose."

This cat, Ampersand, by the way, is a good pictograph of
Robinson's saving sense of humor. Miss Watchman, the
novelist, could not bear to see how beautifully the wrong
world works; one look, and she fell into a heap of dust.
When Atlas took his art too seriously, he went out and
put an end to himself.

There is irony in Robinson's use of the old romantic
names, which once meant whole charters of salvation, on
the small and defeated people of today. Big names are
often hard burdens to bear, the big names that went so
well once in the big houses. Theophilus has more of the
Devil in him than God, he is the man who is at his best
when asleep. Old King Cole planned to settle down to
enjoying old age in Tilbury Town, and he settled down
to making the best of two worthless sons with fine Greek
names. Llewellyn and Priscilla, man and wife, lead a life
that makes their romantic names a mockery. Poor, lonely
Mr. Flood of Tilbury, entertaining himself as the best
and only company he could find, tips his jug up in the

moonlight and drinks. And his creator compares him to "Roland's ghost winding a silent horn." This is the New England recreation of Chivalry.

There remains the greatest irony of all in Robinson's poetry. This poet who wrote early of Miniver Cheevy, who loved Thebes and Camelot, the Medici, and "the medieval grace of iron clothing," himself escaped, in some of his longest and greatest poems, into the old world of Arthur and his knights and ladies. The lover of absolutes, in a modern world that has no room for them, found his happiest characters in an ancient tapestry of human worthiness, in one of the two greatest story cycles the human race has produced. Robinson's Tristram and Iseult and Lancelot are not mere paraphrases of the old Arthurian characters, as all the other modern Arthurian heroes have tended to be; they are tough and unique people. Their doubts and their time sense alone would serve to make them new. But they are studies in love and courage made convincing only by our acceptance of ancient patterns of belief. Belief in man's importance in the universe and to the universe, belief in an ideal of the good, which you can call Platonism if you want to. For many of us today, this amounts to a kind of retreat, rather than a "suspension of disbelief," which all great poems demand of readers. The Arthurian world is the right world, and it is the world Robinson escapes to when he finds his Big-House New England one a ruin. It is like a vast Mac-Dowell Colony, with higher mountains than even Monadnock to wall it round with beauty and keep the small people out.

But that other poet of ours, Robert Frost, has another way of salvation. He does not have to flee into the past. He remains where he is, where his ancestors were before him. His world was never ruined, though it is a New England one. His is the New England of the small house. This Small-House world is too far from the sea and the great towns ever to have built its hopes too much on the wealth that comes in wooden ships, too much on a code hard to live up to. The very sensitive, aristocratic New Englander is fast disappearing, or has fallen on evil days. He is a man who has culture for his blood almost, he must always live out of books as well as out of the earth, and must constantly work to improve himself. But the other old-stock New Englander survives, in all his vigor and toughness. He is the sturdy New Englander who never expected too much, and so was never disappointed, who worked himself into his woods and stonewalls and barns. He stands up now with his feet solidly planted on his ledges, just as tall as ever he was, and keeps an eye on the weather and on men's ways. And he is a well man.

The little ones survive. That can do for the species of animals in the long race for survival. It can do for trees in a gale. It can do for men.

> But when I asked to know what ailed New Hampshire,
> She said she couldn't stand the people in it,
> The little men (it's Massachusetts speaking).
> And when I asked to know what ailed the people,
> She said, "Go read your own books and find out."

There have always been a lot of little people in New Hampshire. That is why it has always been so good a

5

state. Frost is one of the kind he writes about. There have always been a lot of Little-House people in Maine, too. Some of the old Big-House Maine people, my friends and my relations, have learned how to come down in the world, come down in life, come down to life, and get a new grip on the earth and go on being well men. Not only in their hands and feet and head, but in their hearts. A great many Big-House New Englanders everywhere have made this escape into a new world, and they have brought poetry along with them. They have their poets. And their poetry is the poetry of well men.

III

THE POET IN A NEW WORLD

"Poetry is that by which we live forever and ever un-jaded." So Robert Frost says, in a recent letter he wrote me. When one form of the beautiful has lost its power to shape our living every day, we put it carefully away, in an attic or a parlor bookcase, and go out to look for a form that has life in it. If we get tired of the sound of the sea in the polished parlor shell, there is always the real sea to listen to. It is never the same twice. That ocean in the shell is always the same, for it is really in our own brain. The real ocean has other shells, and there is life in them. It is the same with poets. When they discover that their forms are forms of a world that has crumbled away, they put them aside, even though some of them may bear the imprint of a mind as fine as Plato's. An artist in a wrong world must go out and look for a new one. It may be he will not have far to go. Artists cannot be tired men. All great poetry is new. It comes as a surprise, as something to make a man catch his breath to think he has seen these things the poet sees all along and yet has never really seen them!

So it is with the poetry of Robert Frost. To think we have had unwritten poems around us, in all our Mondays and Tuesdays and Wednesdays, and in places right near home! So near home they had become familiar, and we took them for granted. We were looking for poems in books, at the other end of the earth, and in the landscapes of dreams—bad dreams, often—and we had been setting our feet right on them and handling them when we shook hands with a neighbor! And speaking the language of poetry when we talked!

Robert Frost went out of the back door of his little New England farmhouse, and he met a poem before he had got around the corner of the ell. He went around doing the small jobs that never get done on a small farm, the way they get done on one of the big ones in the Middle West; he was farming by hand, he had dirt on his hands; and he picked up poems everywhere. And the whole small farm was flooded with a new kind of light people had not ever noticed before, because they had old eyes. This farmer had a pair of new ones.

And this man's eyes saw the exquisite patterns of rightness in the simplest thing he was doing, setting up the stones in a wall, maybe, or cleaning out last year's leaves from a spring. I know that kind of spring. My father had one on his farm. It is a barrel set in the ground without a bottom, and birch leaves gather clusters of diamonds on their edges where they lie under water, and a moonstone rounds up in the bottom where the water bubbles up. Maybe another jewel hangs in the air, without a thread, where a dragonfly hovers. Robert Frost reminded me that was a poem. And the young calf that tottered when his mother licked him with her tongue!—That was another good one, a sight so common and comforting as that is forever new. The times I had picked blueberries and not known I was kneeling in poetry! I had seen the

morning dewdrops clustered up along with the blueberry
leaves and berries, but I never had known they were such
a beautiful sight as this:

> The fruit mixed with water in layers of leaves,
> Like two kinds of jewels, a vision for thieves.

Axe-handles, grindstones, stone-drags, a bird's nest, a
patch of old snow—they are all poems to this man. Going
for water, plowing and seeding, mowing, rolling apples
down into a cellar, gathering leaves—homely and common everyday chores are rituals of lovely and loyal living
that make a man feel so good that he forgets about trouble
and sorrow and the dying he must come to some day.
Tasks of day to day, year to year; but also life to life
ones. They are like poems full of symbols, when you
come to think of it. And a man doing small farming has
great friends at his elbow: the seasons, frost and rain,
night and day, and others, too. Not the great aristocratic
friends in books, preaching perfection, but the great com-
moners who teach a man how to get along: gladness,
compassion, fear, grief, "he-ness," to bring out the "she-
ness" in a mate; good neighbors for a man who does not
want to be alone, or grow out of the real world into one
he has to build for himself. Frost does not always call
these friends by name. In his fear of absolutes, he often
avoids naming even next-door neighbors like grief and
compassion. But he doesn't need to name them. They are
there.

Frost has written new poems on the ancient art of right
living, the living that is close to seeds falling in the fur-

row and the sap rising in the reddening maple trees.
Here are northern georgics, New England ones. Here is
a new thing under the sun, a New World *rura cano*, nature poetry that is fresh as the sky this morning. It is hard
to believe that a poet could find such newness in things
so old, in so ancient a subject. It seemed that the bucolic
theme was jaded and played out. But here is great poetry .
on country living that makes the old seem still older.
Beside Frost, Hesiod writes mere calendars for ancient
cattle kings and agricultural demigods; the Greek pastoral is the rural living of aristocrats playing like Marie
Antoinette at milking, playing at love and singing;
Horace's rural song seems like that of a tired business
man week-ending in the country; Virgil's, too, seems like
vacation poetry of an urban man, in spite of his having
modern eyes for livestock and bees. Beside Frost's,
Spenser's nature is concocted, and Shakespeare's rusticity,
a game of carving hearts on trees; Herrick's is an archaic
Cavalier slenderness and gaiety, thin notes of old chamber
music. Wordsworth's seems, for all its symphonic magnificence, a country living mixed up with a static morality
and philosophic pattern too old to us to be vital; Wordsworth's people seem too whole and too picturesque and
good to be true. The country loveliness of Keats and
Shelley seems almost theatrically unusual, and too many
human features are on the wind and the clouds, on autumn
and the spring.

Frost has put the real country into words. It is a particular countryside. But its particulars are as creative as
generals in other poets. It is a New England of small,

hilly farms, thin soil, quite a lot of woods, and a few hard-working people who have learned not to expect too much of life. It is a land of hand farming and heart farming. It is a land of *litotes*; that's understatement, in case you have forgotten your old-fashioned rhetoric. It is not a country of easy living. If you are looking for an easy life, beware of the man who deeds you a farm in New Hampshire! He is a Greek bearing gifts. Robert Frost had that happen to him. He finally sold the farm and took the money to go to England and write out a lot of the poems he had been gathering on the hard New Hampshire soil. But he bought another farm in Vermont out of the proceeds of these poems. He put the good he had got out of the land right back into it. "Build soil," is one of Frost's axioms. Building soil is one of the leading occupations on a New England farm. Sweat is one of our best fertilizers. But if our apple crop is small, it makes up for things in taste. We don't raise so much of anything as to become monopolists:

> The only person really soiled with trade
> I ever stumbled on in old New Hampshire
> Was someone who had just come back ashamed
> From selling things in California.

New Hampshire, and Maine, too, have gold, but not in what Frost calls " commercial quantities."

> Just specimens is all New Hampshire has,
> One each of everything as in a show-case
> Which naturally she doesn't care to sell.

But New Hampshire and the other states in the northern tier of New England have many poems that no one had thought to gather into books until Robert Frost came along and began doing it. It has winter. Snow was in the margin of *Snow-Bound*. But it never really came into poetry until Frost put it there. Snow is our leading crop for six or seven months of the year. And winter has a lot to it that can elevate life:

> It lifts existence on a plane of snow
> One level higher than the earth below,
> One level nearer heaven overhead,
> And last year's berries shining scarlet red.

There is a lot of what men once put into their old-fashioned heaven in this "winter Eden" of New England.

> So near to paradise all pairing ends:
> Here loveless birds now flock as winter friends.

For one thing, a long winter makes summer—even a few days of summer—appreciated when it comes. But Frost has poems with as much winter in them as summer. Snow dust sparkles through his verses like his own bright mind. There are plenty other local poems: the fresh ruts in country roads in April, the quick, bright lizards in thawing snow, birches bent over like girls trailing their hair on the grass, blue butterflies that appear all at once out of nowhere on one certain day in spring, as sure as sunrise:

> It is blue-butterfly day here in spring,
> And with these sky-flakes down in flurry on flurry
> There is more unmixed color on the wing
> Than flowers will show for days unless they hurry.

But these are flowers that fly and all but sing:
And now from having ridden out desire
They lie closed over in the wind and cling
Where wheels have freshly sliced the April mire.

Here, too, is a west-running brook in a place where all the others run east—to give a touch of the New England independence and individuality. There are the "flowery waters" of the spring pools, and the hepaticas, the "watery flowers," that look so much like them. Here are trees marching into an unmowed field, here's the feel of a ladder's rung on one's instep long after the apples are picked and put away, when one is lying on the edge of sleep, and pomace on a cow's side-motioned mouth. Here's a maple tree with all her body naked and her scarlet dress all around her feet one late fall morning. Then there's the saying of "Good-bye and keep cold" to the apple trees as winter comes back again. And the thick northern woods are filling up once more with snow. Here's a great plenty of poems for one who has an eye for them. It is as if a poet had opened the old skies and let in a light to show us how our old world is a new world.

It is exact and expert poetry. Frost gets down the right New England names for things: Morgan colts, fox-grapes, stone-boats. We call stone-boats drags in Maine, but the poor New Hampshire farmers, lacking real boats and the ocean, can be forgiven calling the best things they can by the fine name of boat. Frost knows the way the frost overthrows a wall. He knows where things belong. He puts the home burying-ground in the right place. He puts the morning-glories just where they should be, by the back-doorstep, not the front. He knows where menfolks wash up in the kitchen. He knows the French-Canadian English. He knows New England boys; they are rather less boisterous and noisy than other boys and take their pleasures gravely and even sadly. He knows their home-made games. Buckling-Birches, for one. He knows the science of decay in abandoned houses. He knows exactly what goes on on a farm after the people leave, just as surely as he knows it is an azure dust which makes blueberries blue, and if that dust is rubbed off, they will be black. He knows that children stick a flower in their blueberries when they get their pails full. It is the right thing to do. He knows how a good man loads a hayrack, "tagging" each forkful as he puts it on, so he can find each forkful when he unloads, and pitch the hay off without lifting the whole rack each time. Frost knows the rightness and beauty in the handle of an axe, the horse's-hoof knob at the end. And he knows the warm French-Canadian artist in living at the other end of it. This axe-helve takes you into a house and shows you every fine, warm thing there, even to the Canadian woman carrying herself back to her starting place in her rocking-chair. There generally is a man at the other end of things Robert Frost knows best about. He takes his nature with people stuck into it, where they belong. This is expert and exquisite knowledge. It isn't the kind of acquaintance you can strike up in a year or two. It takes a lifetime of keeping your eyes open and getting down on your knees to see, a lifetime of devoted awareness.

Photography merely, as some have maintained?—Not

if you know your head from a grindstone. These things
Frost sees not merely as objects, in three dimensions. They
are objects with tenderness and sensitivity like a nimbus
around them. They mean more than they seem. This is
great art. It is a new kind of vision. You try to find a
camera that can show you how close cousins hepaticas and
spring pools are, both having blueness and both having
wateriness to them. You try to find one! One that will
prove that blue butterflies "are flowers that fly and all but
sing." I'd like to own a camera like that! This is fresh
looking at things in more than three dimensions, looking
at things as if for the first time. It is astounding accuracy,
almost a new science of seeing. Frost uses exquisite realism, but he is not a realist. His heart and his good sense
get too much in his way for that. He might be called a
Monday realist: that is, he believes in the institution of
weekly cleaning. He himself declares he enjoys his potato
best without the dirt. Dirt produces the potato, but it
isn't necessary to eat dirt to get the potato's flavor. The
potato improves on one kind of nature. Frost improves
on several kinds. He likes muck and mire and human
passions that are near the animals' level, not for what
they are, but for what they produce. His admiration rises
as the level of the plant rises, to the flower, to the seed.
This is very different realism from, let us say, James
Joyce's; the movement of admiration is upwards.

I said it is hard to separate Frost's nature from human
nature, his flowers and trees and apples from people, even
stubble-scarred apples from people. He says the same
thing himself. He insists constantly that he is not a na-

ture poet. He calls himself a poet of people. All nature is related to them. Not they to it, as is the way with Wordsworth. He deals with people in the state of nature best—state of *good* nature, I am always tempted to add, remembering Frost's determination—it amounts to that— to see the good points about people rather than their bad. So New England secretiveness is mixed in with blue- berries, and a man who keeps quiet about where the big blueberries grow is forgiven the sin of covetousness for the blueberries' sake. Wall-mending becomes a sermon— Frost would shy away from the word—in neighborliness. A plain farmer gets mixed up with the stars when he takes up a cooled meteor to build into his wall. Frost's particulars everywhere run out to great universals. A man cannot cut a small crop of hay without bringing into his barn something that is dusted with the great laws out in interstellar space. Little human patterns are parts of great starry ones just as surely as Emerson and Whitman repre- sent them. Here is another bold American citizen of the stars; only Frost does not do so much shouting about planets' rights when he goes to the polls to vote. This poet's own pair of old shoes can bring the Atlantic and Pacific together. He wet one in saltwater on Long Island and the other at the Cliff House on the California shore.

> I touch my tongue to the shoes now
> And unless my sense is at fault,
> On one I can taste Atlantic,
> On the other Pacific, salt.

That proves that the wearer of the shoes has covered his
country,
> And got the United States stated.

This is Frost's particular kind of strength. He measures
vastness by the imprint of man doing common human
things. He is the poet of human particulars, and yet his
particulars build up a new kind of symbolism. He avoids
such names as symbolism, when he can, but his poems
have the power of becoming symbols when you read into
them as much trained and careful emotion as Frost put
into their making. Careful emotion is a New Englander's
idea of a right emotion. Tip Frost's stones in a pasture
over, and look at them carefully, and you can see they are
a part of the stellar universe. So one man's careful rumination on the coming of a winter darkness and woods
filling up with snow becomes an analogy of every man's
life and his relation to the whole world, if you want it to.
Only the rumination must not be too lengthy:

> Whose woods these are I think I know.
> His house is in the village though;
> He will not see me stopping here
> To watch his woods fill up with snow.

> My little horse must think it queer
> To stop without a farmhouse near
> Between the woods and frozen lake
> The darkest evening of the year.

> He gives his harness bells a shake
> To ask if there is some mistake.
> The only other sound's the sweep
> Of easy wind and downy flake.

The woods are lovely, dark and deep.
But I have promises to keep,
And miles to go before I sleep,
And miles to go before I sleep.

Woods and night, a snowstorm and a little horse and his master, and a journey to go—they are all parts that fit together into a larger pattern.

Such a thing is called a symphony, I think. This special symphony is all the more remarkable because it comes together, or seems to come together, naturally, without effort on its author's part. But do not be deceived. Behind many of Frost's plain statements of the facts of poetry, there is a disciplined artist who took years to come to his excellence. He takes a long time on each poem now. He is one of the slowest of our poets. In any case, Frost's symphony—and this is another word he would be shy of—seems totally unpremeditated. It unfolds out of itself, and in a new way. Its parts remain so casual and so slender that you may not think the poem is a symphony until long after your first reading, or Frost's first reading of it. Frost generally gives two readings, as those of you know who have heard him read will remember, of the poems he likes best. And he is pretty apt to like his best poems best. That's a pretty fair sign of his greatness, by the way. It takes a great poet to be right in his judgment of his own poems. Robinson had that quality of greatness. For Rollo Walter Brown reports, in his absorbingly pleasant little book about living next door to E. A., that Robinson liked especially *Mr. Flood's Party* and *Isaac and Archibald* and *Tristram*. And almost always the poems that Robert Frost picks out as his best and reads over twice in succession are ones that have this symphonic "togetherness" that I speak of.

And while I am mentioning Frost's reading of his own poems, I should like to take time out to say right here— and I am speaking as a veteran listener to Robert Frost reading—that this man is the best reader of his own work there is. No so honest a voice for poems that are sheer honesty may ever be found again. Bedrock poetry needs a bedrock voice, and this man has it. He makes his lines sound as if they had always been there and he had only taken the pains to pick them up from among the stones of a New England pasture. And yet, especially when Frost reads a poem right over again, the delicate and lovely tissue of related being he has surprised in its hiding place, among the commonest sights and actions, shines out like the lawful concentration of the fine lines in a spider's web on a clear September morning, when there is dew on the web and you can see it all. Right sounds have met right words, and you have a poem that can make you hold in your breath. It is a little net, but its lines are as sure as the patterns that compose the nebulae.

But I must finish my metaphor of the symphony. There are no nice *andantes, prestos, gigues,* and such in succession, it seems. They are all here, but the *adagio* and *scherzo* are often mixed, just the way they are in life. In the lightest of Frost's moments enough seriousness can come suddenly in to set his mind working as well as his belly. I say belly, because Frost believes in having some of his laughs start that low. A laugh with Frost can go a

long ways. It can go high enough to touch even the
totalitarian state. There is his poem *Departmental*:

> An ant on the table cloth
> Ran into a dormant moth
> Of many times his size.
> He showed not the least surprise.
> His business wasn't with such.
> He gave it scarcely a touch,
> And was off on his duty run.
> Yet if he encountered one
> Of the hive's enquiry squad
> Whose work is to find out God
> And the nature of time and space,
> He would put him onto the case.
> Ants are a curious race;
> One crossing with hurried tread
> The body of one of their dead
> Isn't given a moment's arrest—
> Seems not even impressed.
> But he no doubt reports to any
> With whom he crosses antennae,
> And they no doubt report
> To the higher up at court.
> Then word goes forth in Formic:
> "Death's come to Jerry McCormic,
> Our selfless forager Jerry.
> Will the special Janizary
> Whose office it is to bury
> The dead of the commissary
> Go bring him home to his people.
> Lay him in state on a sepal.
> Wrap him for shroud in a petal.
> Embalm him with ichor of nettle.
> This is the word of your Queen."

And presently on the scene
Appears a solemn mortician;
And taking formal position
With feelers calmly atwiddle,
Seizes the dead by the middle,
And heaving him high in air,
Carries him out of there.
No one stands round to stare,
It is nobody else's affair.

It couldn't be called ungentle.
But how thoroughly departmental.

Frost's profession is people. They are a peculiar breed of people. They really have not got into poetry before. Some of them are surprised to be there now. I know that, for I live in the midst of a lot of them. They hardly suppose even yet that they are poetic timber. They had thought refined people were the kind poets wanted to put in their books, dressed-up folks. The way they are themselves on a few special occasions in life, when they are getting married, or showing off the first baby, at the photographer's. Poetry to them means solemnity not untouched with awe. It means special behavior, anyway. But Frost has caught them unawares. They are not, to use the very common idiom, people all dressed up with no place to go. They are in their old clothes and already there. They have places to live in, they are not visiting, as at the photographer's. They are at all sorts of work, not merely in a state of being, like Wordsworth's people, so often. They are totally unconscious both of their vigor and their democracy, unlike Whitman's citizens of " these States."

6

Democracy, did I say?—Yes, most of them have demo-
cratic principles in them. That is, they judge a man by
what he can do, not what he can say. But they also have
immense aristocratic reserves of tenderness and shyness.
For these are New England democrats, and they often
have surprising elements in them. They may believe in
keeping up appearances when they have only one pair of
pants to their name. That's a pretty good test for a Cavalier. For—if we may substitute breeches for trousers—a
man like Sir John Suckling or Richard Lovelace. But
then, remember, they have lived next-door neighbors for
many years to the Big-House people. And a lot of Big-
House people have married into the family. Still, a lot of
Frost's people are no better than they should be. Some
are worse. Some of them are graceless and do not get
ahead in the world, unless it is by burning down the
house for the fire insurance and buying a telescope to
study the stars. But unlike Robinson's people, they almost
never brood or shut themselves away from life. They
stay right in the middle of it. There are none of the
loafers Whitman so admires. They are people who expect adversity and small potatoes and few in a hill. They
are different from folks in Arkansas and California.
Sometimes some of them have a streak of crudeness in
them, but crudeness has its place, as a sort of good sea-
soning, Frost thinks. Though these people go in for horse
laughs and belly laughs, they have quite a lengthy code
of decency. They don't talk about it, but they live up to it.
And each man may have one a bit different from the
others'. This is New England and independence. They

are live-and-let-live philosophers. They don't call themselves by that parlor name. You have to remind them they are philosophers. And they may not always take kindly to your telling them so, as Frost himself shies away from being called parlor names. They are often cranky individualists. They allow for the wind in most things. But they have charity and sentiment, when those things come in their proper order, though they haven't much use for sentimentality. I remember what a lobsterman said once when the summer people he was giving a ride in his boat raved over a sunset and asked him if he didn't think it was gorgeous. "It don't bother me none," he said. The funny thing was, as I happen to know, he does like sunsets. That's why he said it. The accent should be on *bother*.

Robert Frost learned something from Wordsworth and even more from Crabbe, in getting his training in looking for the right kind of people to go into his kind of poem. But he learned best by being one of the particular kind of people he was looking for. And he improves on Crabbe in writing of rural human beings; he leaves out the whine and the sneer.

If I had to choose one outstanding instance of Frost's expert and yet tender understanding of rural New England human beings, I could not do better than choose his hired help. Now New England hired men are not like hired men anywhere else. They are the aristocrats of all paid help. They are a very superior order of human beings. "Thrones, Dominations, Princedoms, Virtues, Powers"—so ran the descending orders of rulers in heaven. On a New England farm it would run: Farmer, hired men, old aunts and uncles, aunts and uncles who are younger, hired girls, wife, and children. The hired men are next to their masters. They have to be treated even more tactfully than masters. I know what I am talking about, for I was brought up among a lot of princes, a lot of hired men, on a farm. They had to have the best at table, had to be waited on first; they had to be consulted with and not given orders, they had to be humored and honored in the fields. They ordered the boys of the family to toe the line as a father never could order them. I know of a case where all the hired men, one hay-time, left a farm in a body when the woman of the house would not sit down at table with them. That was in Vermont. But Maine is about the same. Frost's poem, *The Code,* can tell you better than I can about this race of superior beings. A New Hampshire farmer sinned against a law of not "bulling" his help. We call that "crowding" in Maine. But it's all the same thing. That farmer kept at a hired man until the unloading in the barn, and when he said, "Let her come," he got a whole rackful of hay on him in ten lots. He got out from under. But he had to warm his feet in the oven the hottest day of summer, to get over the scare. He didn't say anything to the hired man. He knew he himself had sinned. He didn't go back with the men the rest of the day. He picked a mess of peas for his wife.

There were good reasons for all the tremendous code of diplomacy built up about hired men. They were of the farmer's own stock usually, his own equals, and often his own relations. As men temporarily or permanently without the substance of overlordship, they demanded a tenderer respect for their inborn New England pride. The permanently landless were like Lucifer just before the Fall. Fictions of their importance had to be created and preserved. It is such a fiction for one of the tiredest and shabbiest and proudest of this now vanishing race that Robert Frost uses in, maybe, the tenderest and most moving of modern tragedies, *The Death of the Hired Man.* The little fiction of this man's importance was all he had left in the world, now that his arms and legs, as well as his brother, had failed him. He came home. You may recall Frost's New England definition of home:

> Home is the place where, when you have to go there,
> They have to take you in.

He crept home to his real home, his old place of work, to die in the faint warmth of it. Such a fiction is great enough to take the place of the ancient estate of kingship and make a New England hired man a brother of the ancient great.

Through these people of Frost's the essential New England has emerged at last, the tough and lasting New England. New England has always been more famous for making people than for making shoes and sheets. Now that the shoes and sheets have gone elsewhere to be made, the leading occupation of the place shows up more clearly. And the new stocks furnish about as good examples of the product as the English stocks did. You can raise better boys than you can potatoes on a New

Hampshire farm. They can get around the ledges better, and get more nourishment out of them. This tough New England has always been there. Frost merely discovered it first. The trouble with Whittier and Longfellow was that they carried around too many books when they went looking for these poetic people of Frost's. They didn't have time to use their eyes and ears and sit down and talk and discover them properly. These people were there just the same as their blueberries and birches were. The older writers just didn't see their poetic possibilities. When they did use these people at all, it was for lighter poems and *genre* poems. They took the greatest pains to misspell their talk to make it look humorous. And the poets condescended, as Lowell in his *Biglow Papers.* That's one thing you can't do with men and women like these. It's the New England unpardonable sin.

And rightly and expertly put into poetry, these people, for all their sharp corners and crab-like ideas of going ahead backwards or sideways, become proper and universal common people. They have such toughness and lasting human nature in them. In being one of them and putting them into books for the world to read, Frost is being a first-rate proletarian poet. A warm one, a live one. He does not get on bandwagons or make speeches or sign up for political purposes. Politics are only a part of proletarianism. Frost likes his people in individuals, not mass formation. He isn't blaming their troubles on the capitalists or the environment, but on the way life is built and the way they are built. It is a wider kind of idealism. And, anyway, troubles may be good for a man. Frost has found it so.

Frost is the real radical among modern poets. Men like E. E. Cummings and T. S. Eliot are the pseudo-radicals. The pseudo-ones get the most space in the papers and with the critics. That is usually the way with the smaller radicals. They are radicals who leave out capitals and punctuation marks, or, as is the case of James Joyce and T. S. Eliot, in their most typical books, *Ulysses* and *The Waste Land*, they pursue the novelty of grafting healthy tissue on to dead. They take the healthiest myths the race has yet created—the myths of Telemachus and Odysseus and Arthur, and they graft them upon the dull and ingeniously jaded living by the day in gray Dublin or London houses. And there you have something new in the way of mysticism! Actually, much of the matter and the imagination of the pseudo-radicals, separated from the novelties of parody, word-twisting, and psychopathic abnormality, is jaded and stuffy Victorian material as dated as plush furniture. Frost himself has something to say on the methods of the pseudo-radicals. He says it in his Introduction to Robinson's last poem, *King Jasper*. "The one old way to be new no longer served. Science put it into our heads that there must be new ways to be new. Those tried were largely by subtraction— elimination. Poetry, for example, was tried without punctuation. It was tried without capital letters. It was tried without metric frame on which to measure the rhythm. It was tried without any images but those to the eye. . . . It was tried without content under the trade name of poesie pure. It was tried without phrase, epigram, coherence, logic and consistency. It was tried without ability. . . . Robinson stayed content with the old-fashioned way to be new." That is the way of being new and understood, at the same time. Frost has taken that way, without declaration of independence from the old. For he preserves what is best in the old as all the great poets, who are also the new poets, do. A good part of what is best in the old, is, as he puts it, fear of man and fear of God.

With these two at either hand, Robert Frost has not been afraid to take down a piece of the wall of the sky and let in a light which shows us that the small, old, New England farm world he had lived in so snugly is a tremendously wide and new place, full of a radiance that transforms the common houses and hills, full of fresh poetic people living by the old and everlasting principles of right living, living up to a belief in something greater than themselves, living up to a belief in something that many neighbors add up to, living not by the day but by the lifetime, and by a wider standard than a lifetime. He has shown us that beauty is forever young and fresh and new.

This poet has helped other poets to open their eyes to this new world. I, for one, have learned from this man more about where and how to look for poems than from any of the older poets. There's Malam in Vermont, and Hillyer and Holmes in Massachusetts. And there's Wilbert Snow in Maine. Snow goes and finds his poems among fishermen, as Frost finds his among farmers. But the Maine poet finds much the same kind of poems. Clam-diggers and lobstermen have come into poetry along with Frost's inland workaday men. Here also are proletarians, and ones that do not go out of date with the passing of the centuries.

And the other New England poet whom I have chosen for these lectures, though he has not found a world so wide and new as Frost, has found, for his shorter, early poems at least, new men and women who had never been taken up into poetry before. Mr. Flood is one, being courteous and gentle with himself in his old age, with his jug under the two moons. Aunt Imogen is another, who, for all her bare spinster's life, had one moment's feeling of being a god and suffering like one when she crushed a small boy to her heart. It is something new to have poems made out of such lonely and defeated people, people who are more real than some of the ancient great who had kingdoms to lose. For these people have no such kingdoms to lose any more. They and the faceless people in Robinson's longer poems are all the more tragic because they settle nothing and point no moral when they go down in defeat. They go down like a last surviving member of a baffled race called men, like one who walks into the fire of the sunset sky.

But Frost's people are not people of defeat and the sunset. They are people of the sunrise.

IV

A NEW LANGUAGE FOR POETRY

"'Poetry is the renewal of words forever and ever. Poetry is that by which we live forever and ever unjaded. Poetry is that by which the world is never old. Even the poetry of trade names gives the lie to the unoriginal who would drag us down in their own powerlessness to originate. Heavy they are but not so heavy that we can't rise under them and throw them off.'"

My quotation comes from a recent letter of Frost's to me. His statements are the answer he makes to the frequent enough declaration of critics, lately, that our world has grown old, that people are tired, and their languages worn out. It is one of Frost's talk subjects, this on language, he calls it *The Renewal of Words*. It is necessary for the poet who has discovered a new world to find new words and new arrangements of them. One of the most precious things in the world, according to Robert Frost, is "correspondence." All human beings, from the cradle, crave to be understood. In poets the craving should be stronger than in common men. "Mind must convince mind that it can uncurl and wave the same filaments of subtlety, soul convince soul that it can give off the same shimmers of eternity." Robert Frost, from being good friends with his early, rural neighbors, has grown into a man who wants to be friends with all the world. It is a part of his creed of neighborliness. It is expanded

74

neighborliness. And great poets are great neighbors to the world. Some of the most discussed modern poets are anything but that. They are not even good neighbors with themselves. And most of the fault is their own, for they have deliberately turned to a private kind of poetry. Their words are not oratory—that is, they do not try to convince people of anything. These poets have shut themselves up in the dark, in unintelligibility, in moodiness and contempt of people. That is why many of them are jaded and bored men or men of despair. They have used their words against themselves. They have lifted them up like walls around them. For such men language *is* jaded, for it has lost its reason for being.

"Poetry is the renewal of words."—That is a kind of brief history of English poetry. For the long road the English poets have come has always been full of the danger of dying words. Words are bad enough, dead; but the phrases they make up are even more so when they are dead. Worse still are dead rhythms and metrical forms. And the worst of all things that can happen is the dying of imagery. These four things: the words, the phrases, the prosody, and the image are the ascending steps, I believe, in the stairway of poetic language. And when the bottom step has crumbled, when words have lost their savor, it is with language as with stairways, the rest falls to ruin, too. We have seen this happen more than once. The Elizabethans wore out their bright Renaissance words, wore out their witty phrases and ingenious parallelisms, they overworked the sonnet and pastoral, and their Petrarchan conceits grew stale. And even as the latter Elizabethans were playing an empty game with words, John Donne and Ben Jonson came up, robust and fresh from living in multitudinously virile and exciting ways. The one brought in strange new words from science and sex and alchemy and contemporary geography and medicine, brought in prosy and crotchety phrases, new verse forms, and an imagery that combines the flesh and the spirit, to interrelate all parts of created life, in stones and men and stars. So the seventeenth century metaphysical poetry was born. The other revolutionist, Ben Jonson, brought into English verse the severity and poverty of the ancient Classical poets, reduced images to economical proportions and sharp exactness, and wrote poems as if he had to be saving of precious materials and were writing in gold letters on marble. He made a love song the length of an epitaph. So the seventeenth century Cavalier lyric began.

At the close of the eighteenth century, the world was strewn once more with dead words and phrases, dead couplets and images that were formulas. And so there was a call for a Blake and a Burns, a Wordsworth and a Coleridge. Commoner words and stranger words came into poetry, the phrase and the image became rich and wild. And once more at the end of the nineteenth century and on into the beginning of ours, we find the rich and wild poetic style wearing out into sheer incantation and wizardry of sound in Swinburne and later men. The Imagists broke some old forms up, but they invented still older. They went about the matter of supplying new images and phrasing in the wrong, in the artificial way, and so opened the road to later and queerer intellectual experimenters, such as the Objectivists and all the rest. And while the Imagists were making a beginning at the wrong end of the stairs—with the phrases and images and not with the words—two men, independently, had begun the poetic revolution and had discovered a language that was alive. It is almost a demonstration of Providence, at this late day, that Robinson and Frost came when they did.

These two poets brought a new simplicity, new plainness and bareness, almost, into the wording of poetry. It is a language very close to what men speak now, a language without gestures and without intonations, whether of grandeur or pathos. These poets keep their hands at their sides—if I may use such a figure—when they speak. And they do speak in the lines of their poems. Their discovery of the power of simplicity and of natural speaking is all the more important, it seems to me, because they made it independently, and because they did not issue any preface to any lyrical ballads about it. They came naturally by their power, and they used it naturally. They did not make up creeds or write dogmatically about it. Both Robinson and Frost are quiet poets. Often the great ones are. They never had to preach their newness. If other, lesser innovators were given more space in the critical literature, they were content to go on being new without having it announced from the pulpit every Sunday morning.

Indeed, Robinson's being caught up, after years of quiet neglect, as a sort of standard bearer of the revolution of

1915, was a thing that seemed rather to surprise and amuse him. He never bore any standard, of course; he was contented to go on being a poet. That took all his time. And he avoided the spotlight that the noisier radicals tried to bring to bear on him. He was a shy man, and every kind of notoriety appalled him. He was happy, of course, in waking up and finding America reading him instead of a few friends who had been reading him before. He was naïvely glad to make his living comfortably, at last, by poetry. He never ceased to wonder at it. But he never regarded himself as a preacher of a new order. He went on writing the language he had always written, severe, plain, at times rising to a sudden shining phrase, doubling back with a modest doubt, with much of the sound of the human voice in his words and more of the sound of the human brain when it is at the intricate process called thinking.

It was no accident, of course, that Robinson and Frost brought in the plainer style in poetry. There was something in the air, something in the times, something in the tide, that willed it so. The tide had turned. Thanks to science—and it is good to be able to thank science for some assistance to poetry, when we can find so many things in it to hurt the poetical spirit!—thanks to the increased complexity of living, thanks to an improvement in men's wish as well as means to communicate better, man to man, nation to nation; thanks to all these and a thousand other subtle changes, the tide had set, around the beginning of our century, towards a plainer way of speaking. And such a change in the tide demanded plainer speaking in the art of poetry. Compare almost any modern poetry with that of the last century, and you can see at once, I think, how plainness and directness, and even frankness, have increased.

But these men, Frost and Robinson, did not get all their virtue out of thin air or a change in the tide of men's tastes generally. Robinson, and especially Frost, got an idea of looking for poems in people's talk. Talk has always been a feeder of poetry. Witness the old ballads' folk style. There is such a thing as oral literature, and it is all around us, even now when the radio fills the air with talk that is mostly written or talk only on its best behavior. No profane words, I believe, are allowed, the more's the pity—on the speaker's part, that is! Talk ought not always to be under the handicap of being on its best behavior. This oral poetry I speak of as existing around us is a theme of mine that I want to write a book on some day. Oral prose idiom is full of poetry. I haven't listened to talk of Maine fishermen and farmers all these years for nothing. I know that everyday speech is full of fire and music. Weather saws, proverbs of every kind. Figures of speech, metaphors and similes, even—what are those fearful names?—synecdoches and metonymies—are coming out every minute when a man is resting from mowing or plowing, or from pulling a lobster-pot. The man doesn't know it, of course, it would scare him to death if he did. This is literature in the making. A poet's ear can hear poems there. Robinson and Frost, especially, have that kind of ear. "The cat killed by care." It isn't the words alone, or the imagery only, it is the rise and

fall of the voice, the nice word in the right place. These
two poets found a lot of what they have written in this
unwritten literature all about us.

And, of course, and in the third and last place, Frost
and Robinson are that kind of men. I mean they have
minds that run towards sincerity and plainness and a
more than usual New England desire to say things
straight.

Anyway, Frost and Robinson have brought new life
into our poetry. The new life is partly in the words
themselves, many of them such as no Victorian poet
would dream of using as being too exact, too much to
the point, and too bread-and-buttery. It would be a shock
to Tennyson and Swinburne to read many of Robinson's
Arthurian lines. The flowery fictions spread around men's
best emotions, blurred out purposely in the older poetry,
have given way to needle words and tooth words, and
Robinson often bites to the quick with his utterly frank
phrasing. He is closer, in his Arthurian poems, to Malory
than to Tennyson. But it is a modern kind of common-
ness and exactness. Neither of our poets allows words
to get in the way of his emotion. That is a token of life.

But these two have also done vast things to the upper
stairs of poetry. Their phrases are shorter and more stac-
cato than those in older English verse. Nor do they
measure them so carefully foot by foot, line by line. They
run over more. They use no lengthy norm of rhythm.
They break and change their rhythm as their moods
change. In general, too, they have gone back to the older-
than-Victorian stanza and poem patterns, to simpler, bal-

ladic patterns, or invented new ones somewhat like them. Frost has gone back to Chaucerian octosyllabic couplets. But his octosyllabics are peculiarly his own—as are many of his pentameter lines—from his habit of using a good many grace notes in every line. One can hardly measure these feet as dactyls or anapests. They are not really such at all. These quick feet of Robert Frost's are talk. And talk as old as the hills and as young as the rain. For they are the lines a New Hampshire blueberry picker lets out of his mouth when he is resting and feeling well; and they are also the feet English poets used to write, in Langland's day still and in earlier, Anglo-Saxon times, before Frenchified men had corrupted English poetry by bringing in measure by foot. They are *beat* lines, not *feet* lines. The kind in *Mother Goose*. They are a man talking.

What these two greatest masters of modern blank verse have done to that ancient, and perhaps most English, of all poetic patterns, is a good, fair sample of their achievement of new life in poetic style generally. We had thought blank verse had had its last variations rung, by poets such poles apart as Shakespeare and Wordsworth. And now come new masters. The Earl of Surrey would find himself at home in their lines, for both Robinson and Frost can, when the occasion demands, write flat prose in blank verse. But even Milton would have to admire passages in *The Death of the Hired Man* and *King Jasper*. For these two make a solemn music all their own, when it suits them to do so. Sparingly. Only now and then. But then, life is less solemn now. The almost

7

complete disappearance of the *caesura*, to mention one technical detail, has made a tremendous change. But something has happened to the ends of the lines; they not only run over, they leap and hop. And when you come to the words and phrases themselves, you can see how endlessly possible the patterning of emotion is. These men have given new life to poets yet to be born.

Never shall I forget, long as I live,
The quaint thin crack in Archibald's voice,
The lonely twinkle in his little eyes,
Or the way it made me feel to be with him.
I know I lay and looked for a long time
Down through the orchard and across the road,
Across the river and the sun-scorched hills
That ceased in a blue forest, where the world
Ceased with it.   Now and then my fancy caught
A flying glimpse of a good life beyond—
Something of ships and sunlight, streets and singing,
Troy falling, and the ages coming back,
And ages coming forward: Archibald
And Isaac were good fellows in old clothes,
And Agamemnon was a friend of mine;
Ulysses coming home again to shoot
With bows and feathered arrows made another,
And all was as it should be.   I was young.

So I lay dreaming of what things I would,
Calm and incorrigibly satisfied
With apples and romance and ignorance,
And the still smoke from Archibald's clay pipe.
There was a stillness over everything,
As if the spirit of heat had laid its hand
Upon the world and hushed it; and I felt

Within the mightiness of the white sun
That smote the land around us and wrought out
A fragrance from the trees, a vital warmth
And fullness for the time that was to come,
And a glory for the world beyond the forest.
The present and the future and the past,
Isaac and Archibald, the burning bush,
The Trojans and the walls of Jericho,
Were beautifully fused; and all went well
Till Archibald began to fret for Isaac
And said it was a master day for sunstroke.
That was enough to make a mummy smile,
I thought; and I remained hilarious,
In face of all precedence and respect,
Till Isaac (who had come to us unheard)
Found he had no tobacco, looked at me
Peculiarly, and asked of Archibald
What ailed the boy to make him chirrup so.
From that he told us what a blessed world
The Lord had given us.

This is a tissue of beauty just as surely as Barabas' cata-
logue of jewels or Faustus' cries to God as a clock ticks
away his hours left on earth. A common farmer and his
wife speak poetry when they are talking one night of their
returned hired man:

"*I* can't think Si ever hurt anyone."

"No, but he hurt my heart the way he lay
And rolled his old head on that sharp-edged chair-back.
He wouldn't let me put him on the lounge.
You must go in and see what you can do.
I made the bed up for him there to-night.
You'll be surprised at him—how much he's broken.
His working days are done; I'm sure of it."

"I'd not be in a hurry to say that."

"I haven't been. Go, look, see for yourself.
But, Warren, please remember how it is:
He's come to help you ditch the meadow.
He has a plan. You mustn't laugh at him.
He may not speak of it, and then he may.
I'll sit and see if that small sailing cloud
Will hit or miss the moon."

                    It hit the moon.
Then there were three there, making a dim row,
The moon, the little silver cloud, and she.

Warren returned—too soon, it seemed to her,
Slipped to her side, caught up her hand and waited.

"Warren?" she questioned.

                    "Dead," was all he answered.

These men can do new things, things that Marlowe and
Shakespeare could not do. They can talk and think, as
Shakespeare and Marlowe could only think and sing.
The two of them can sing even—very briefly, as becomes
their times—except when Robinson is in the latter part
of *Tristram*. There the singing goes on and on, only—
remarkable to note—in phrases as exact as prose. Here,
in the blank verse of Robinson and Frost, is oratory still,
it is writing that has the aim of conviction, and it is all
the more moving because it is unforced, unfictioned, and
full of a natural morality of simple design.

The language of Robinson is one of the most creative
characteristics of his work. If his spirit is often discour-
aged and if he finds the old wholeness of life impossible
in a world too much given to the perfection of pumps

and the substance of things, he speaks his discouragement in a language that is itself an act of faith in life, a tongue full of wonderful accuracy in expression and observation, with phrases and images fresh as May. His words and phrases are ones no poet has used before, in his way. Many of them are ones he must have taken into his mind, as a boy and a young man, in places along the Kennebec, hearing people talk. A lot of the expressions are still there by the river. Robinson was a listener rather than a talker even then, as he was later. His ear was probably the sharper for that. Being built quiet himself, he had plenty of chance to hear life going on in others. And that is one of the best places to look for life going on, in people who do not know they are being recorded and who let life come out of their lips. If they know you are taking down what they are saying, they will stop saying anything, though not always stop talking. There is a good deal of living going on in what people say, in spite of what Hemingway and other artists in two-dimensional talk maintain. There is often an exquisite pattern of reward and retribution, a pattern of morality, being born there where people meet and exchange words. This can happen even among very common people. And being quietly observant, too, Robinson had the chance to look at the carpet of the world and see designs there, in the color and shape of day and night, in the shape of even small creatures and leaves and grass blades. There is freshness there always, and the colors are never the same; different people will see different things if they do not listen too much to the directions given in books as to what to see. So in his idioms and the substance of his imagery, Robinson is the unjaded Robinson, the renewer of language, and, back of the language—it is always so—the renewer of life.

Plain, everyday life furnished this poet with plain idioms. Such, for instance, as these from a small boy's mouth mostly: "I got up and went," "I was ready to sweat blood," "cool to his hat-band," "it was high time those oats were cut," "the warmth and wonder of the land," "scorching days," "my mouth was full of words," "a right smart walk," "out of the fiery sunshine to the gloom," "snowed up for ten days," "take my nerves and tie them in a knot,"

> I'm half afraid you cut those oats of yours
> A day or two before they were well set.

This is an awareness to people who are aware of the earth and making their living out of it, caught in the act. Robinson's words are full of human nature, and the nature comes out explicitly. He writes of the "adhesiveness" of a small boy with an older person. He puts a finger exactly on an impression:

> A story you have read
> In childhood and remembered for the pictures.

Here are homely and convincing parts of life, not fancy creations of a poet's brain. Things everybody has a chance to see, and so few people do. Small things which, at first thought, everyone might say, but no one has said them quite so well as this quiet poet. He notices, too, the smaller inhabitants of the world than men, and he describes their virtues in the same concise and exact and common words:

> I was wondering what made the Lord
> Create a thing so nervous as an ant.

Or

> a cricket, of the brown soft sort
> That feeds on darkness.

And

> a twinging little difference
> That nips you like a squirrel's teeth.

One of the amazing things about the poet Robinson is his combination of intense concentration upon dark, emotional stress and his clean-cut, homely imagery by which he follows its complex progress. Vague and boundless agonies, and. yet the words to them are usually simple ones, and the images exact and common. In his last poem, *King Jasper*, he has a setting that is almost a myth, and his characters are regal, a king and his queen, the prince and his wife, Zoë—whose name and actions are well-nigh allegorical—and an aristocratic avenger of his father, Hebron. There are citizens in the kingdom, somewhere vaguely below the dreamlit royal house; they are growing rebellious. But they never appear. The oppressive air of the castle is full of unseen hands at work on some dim masterpiece of destruction. There are allusions to chimneys that smoke below, but it is a dragon breathing through them. A large part of the action is a dream. Everything borders on symbolism of the obscurest kind. A fierce life-and-death struggle is going on. But it is a

battle of a few lonely figures in the dark. Yet all through
this tissue of dark symbolism runs a bright strand of sharp
images. The king is

> a small, tight man,
> With eyes that should have seen you in the dark.

His face is impassive,

> You may throw billiard balls or bricks at it,
> And they will leave no mark.

Chimneys are called hollow trees on fire. The princess is
described as a wasp, well able

> To sting the mightiest spiders of convention
> And fly away from them as free as ever.

The king is held by a sound of laughter as a bird is held
by a cat. A ghost declares he will mount and ride the
king's shoulders as easily as a squirrel. A very small
chance is

> Almost as large as a mosquito's ears.

There is a plain and almost vulgar figure. Hebron looks
at the princess

> till she wondered
> If all her clothes were on.

But a delicate one, too:

> You would not injure an anemone.

Things are as clear "as a new moon." And another lovely
and peaceful figure comes from nature:

> Humming above me like an earnest bee,
> Who cannot find his way out through a window
> That will not open for him.

If Robinson had been able to find in men's thoughts the clarity and freshness that he puts into his imagery, the mold of sadness could never have contained him. Yet his doubts and agonies are the more impressive against this bright background of belief in nature's forms.

It is one of the attributes of his greatness, surely, that Robinson is able to put the great and the small together. He links Archibald and Isaac with ancient heroes, and puts new life into both sets of men. Perhaps the loveliest instance of Robinson's habit of mixing the high with the low, the splendid with the homely and usual, comes at the end of this same poem. The boy dreams of Archibald and Isaac as two old angels playing High-Low-Jack!

> They had wings,
> And they were sitting where a silver light
> Suffused them, face to face. The wings of one
> Began to palpitate as I approached,
> But I was yet unseen when a dry voice
> Cried thinly, with unpatronizing triumph,
> "I've got you, Isaac: high, low, jack, and the game."

The angels in *Paradise Lost* are not so fresh as these, or human! This is a renewing of angels, as well as a renewal of words. This is a lovely language for a poet in a new world.

Robert Frost has done even greater things than Robinson in giving poetry the life of new words and new metaphors, words and metaphors that can create life. Yet Robert Frost began his wisdom in words by being afraid of them. The fear of words is on him still, I think, today. He is afraid of words getting the upper hold on him.

He is afraid that words will betray him into saying more than he feels. This is the kind of fear Scripture speaks of as being the beginning of wisdom. Because he is a New Englander, he naturally does not believe in showing deep emotion too readily. New Englanders do not wear their hearts on their sleeves, any more than they put their wash in the front yard. They wear their hearts behind their ribs, where hearts belong. But Frost's fear of words goes deeper than that. It is the sign of one of the sincerest men living. It has made him the great artist in words that he is. His fear of too easy words has made him a master at choosing the right ones. I remember one day when I turned Robert Frost loose on a class of mine at college. He lectured the students on the need of their being always on guard against letting beautiful words take the place of even plain thinking. I never told him, but I had been drilling that class for months to begin with provocative phrases of my dictation and to see if the phrases would create poems. I was young then, you see, as a teacher of poetry! Frost taught me and my pupils a lesson we will never forget. Frost is especially afraid of old words and phrases; he thinks they are dead words and phrases. That is why he takes so many words warm off the lips of men.

I believe it is this fear of dead words that makes Frost afraid of another thing: the academy and the academic. Because schools are so often the repositories of the dead languages and the dead poetry of former generations of men, Frost fears them. He comments, in his *Education by Poetry: a Meditative Monologue*, on the fact that many colleges bar American poetry and contemporary poetry from their curriculums. And he says this with something less than his usual smile, maybe, the smile which he usually wears when making extemporary and bold remarks on the central interest of his life, the art of poetry. He takes the edge off this a little by citing the merry instance of a minister's turning his daughter out of his house because she wrote poetry, because he didn't believe in having any more books made: "God wrote one book, and that was enough." But Frost's feeling against colleges still rankles. And Frost believes that when most colleges do teach poetry, of any age, they teach it as almost everything but what it really is: as science, as language, as grammar. To Frost, it is not even the artistic, rhythmic expression of emotion. It is the expression of life. A hard course to find in any curriculum, one in life! It is a course in life with him, this experience of poetry; it ought to be so with others. But what do colleges usually teach in poetry courses? Frost is afraid that it is something more harmful than helpful. Harmful, that is, to the person who is aiming to be a poet. I remember Frost's telling me once, in one of the all-night talks which he is so famous for and which he has made a memorable feature of his friends' lives, how much he was afraid a boy who had it in him to write poetry might be hurt by college. It might blight his natural knowledge of people's nature and nature itself, and substitute knowledge of too many books and too many ideas at second hand. These are the fears of a man who, during more than a decade, has taught in a college. But, again, these are fears that are like the beginning of wisdom.

Frost is hard on college education. Harvard did not mean much to him, any more than it meant much to Robinson. E. A. once spoke out sharply to Rollo Brown on the subject of the emptiness of Harvard professors in his day there. "Stuffed shirts," I think he called them. And as for Frost, some of his hardness of opinion about colleges may well have come into being as a defense against criticism of his ways of teaching which he may have encountered. And doubtlessly Frost is hard on the college, too, because he went to a very fine college, finer even than Harvard, called life. He may well have something of the prejudice of a self-made man. In that institution of higher education, life, he underwent the stern disciplines of hard and tedious work. These disciplines may be achieved also—in all fairness to colleges be it said!—in a stern course in Latin grammar, as well as on a New Hampshire farm. Frost learned in life the lessons of silence and independence and sincerity, and the greater lesson of joy in creating something durable out of the sight and feeling of a moment. But surely the examples of great integrity and great living beyond the measure of the moment, in the poetry of the past, have some power to inspire men to exercise what powers they have to approach living as an art, and, even if they do not create poetry, to read it with more understanding and sympathy. It all depends on how the teaching of poetry is done in college.

Frost admits as much by his own methods at Amherst.

He speaks of them in his *Education by Poetry*. His fears about college teaching have made him careful to keep his subject alive. He tries to guide his students rather than instruct them, to encourage them to take the first steps which may lead ultimately to "great thoughts, grave thoughts, thoughts lasting to the end." The natural way is from the little to the vast. A good deal can be done to make good readers of poetry, if not poets. Frost tries to make such readers. His aim is to arouse young men to experience poetry for themselves. Of course, good taste and good judgment are parts of the training, and metaphor, too. But the student must take care that the metaphor is a part of his life before he uses it. Frost mistrusts marking; he listens for the one thoughtful remark a student may make about poetry which will prove that he has felt something of its power at last. He grades by that one remark. He is suspicious of number. One phrase may mean more than mountains of statistics. Frost, as a professor, does not profess to make poets. He is especially fearful of encouraging mediocrity. "Some people think I want people to write poetry, but I don't; that is, I don't necessarily. I only want people to write poetry if they want to write poetry. I have never encouraged anybody to write poetry that did not want to write it, and I have not always encouraged those who did want to write it. That ought to be one's own funeral. It is a hard, hard life, as they say." He knows it is not possible to make poets, it is only possible to suggest to one who has already the makings of being a poet to go on. Frost is there to set an example. It is ridiculous to expect that "a poet in residence"—the phrase that has been coined for Frost and other poets now on college faculties—will inspire an undergraduate poetic "renaissance." Poets come a few to a century, and wide apart. Number has place in the sciences, not in the arts. Frost is afraid of a city that is full of poets, like one he knows of in the West.

This honesty in teaching is a part of Frost's honesty as a poet. His honesty as a poet shows sometimes in a deliberate choice of words that are so exact or so realistic and hard that they can hardly be called poetical. Some of his poems are surprisingly difficult to read fluently. But then, fluency is a thing to fear, and it is a thing of far less importance than an idea. I should like to read a poem of Frost's as an example of a poem that is an idea poem only, rather than a poem both in idea and words:

Neither Out Far Nor In Deep

The people along the sand
All turn and look one way.
They turn their back on the land.
They look at the sea all day.

As long as it takes to pass
A ship keeps raising its hull;
The wetter ground like glass
Reflects a standing gull.

The land may vary more; *
But wherever the truth may be—
The water comes ashore,
And the people look at the sea.

---

* Incidentally, this line, in an earlier version of this poem, written by Frost in my copy of his *Collected Poems*, reads:
Some say the land has more;
I think it is significant that Frost wrote a more difficult line originally.

They cannot look out far.
They cannot look in deep.
But when was that ever a bar
To any watch they keep?

Frost is a poet so honest that he deliberately avoids easy rhythms and usual and expected music. There is one poem of his in which I think he took pains to break up the effect of inevitable cadence and flow with almost prosy lines. It is his poem *The Last Mowing*:

There's a place called Far-away Meadow
We never shall mow in again,
Or such is the talk at the farmhouse:
The meadow is finished with men.
Then now is the chance for the flowers
That can't stand mowers and plowers.
It must be now, though, in season
Before the not mowing brings trees on,
Before trees, seeing the opening,
March into a shadowy claim.
The trees are all I'm afraid of,
That flowers can't bloom in the shade of;
It's no more men I'm afraid of;
The meadow is done with the tame.
The place for the moment is ours
For you, oh tumultuous flowers,
To go to waste and go wild in,
All shapes and colors of flowers,
I needn't call you by name.

Frost may sometimes be as hard on music as he is on the academic. But this can be set down to the honesty of the man.

And this scrupulousness in choosing the living words,

the exact words, the right words, has led to a power in Frost sometimes as great as Milton's. Milton was an artist at putting new life into words. Some of his Latinate words are more Latin than the words Virgil and Horace used. For Milton went back to the primitive vigor, the figurativeness in the ancient Latin stems. So he describes the fall of the wicked angels from heaven as a *ruin*; he writes that the coils of the Serpent moved *redundant* on the grass. And Milton also uses English words as though they were real objects and very much alive, in such phrases as "*tanned* haycocks" and "*checkered* shade," and the bee with "*honeyed* thigh." Milton is such a poet as can write the whole history of Egypt in one phrase of three words, "the unshowered grass." This is a nation built by a river, not by rainfall. Frost can do tremendous things with a single word, a word that, like some of Milton's, may have cost a week of thought. Such a one is his *loveless*, in the line,

> Here loveless birds now flock as winter friends.

Such another is *watery* in describing hepaticas and anemones. Another is *lariat*, for a wild grapevine. A good axe-helve *cocks* its head. There are Frost's

> bags full of leaves
> As light as balloons,

his *dark intent*, for an angry Pacific Ocean at evening time. Wild flowers are *tumultuous*. These are words you have to think *around*; they create a sudden whole world of sympathy never guessed at before, a world of four dimensions. These are words that are alive, and the sign of great poetry.

With all his plainness and zeal for simplicity, there is in Frost an amazing tenderness and delicacy of fancy. You see it in *Spring Pools*:

> These pools that, though in forests, still reflect
> The total sky almost without defect,
> And like the flowers beside them, chill and shiver,
> Will like the flowers beside them soon be gone,
> And yet not out by any brook or river,
> But up by roots to bring dark foliage on.
>
> The trees that have it in their pent-up buds
> To darken nature and be summer woods—
> Let them think twice before they use their powers
> To blot out and drink up and sweep away
> These flowery waters and these watery flowers
> From snow that melted only yesterday.

This tenderness is as much from the paralleled fall of the phrases as from the lovely exactness of the idea. Frost is capable of great fancy. His fancy can be almost feminine. He writes of trying the new moon like a jewel in his hair, of being afraid for the flowers in the shade of the trees. But his fancy is also as masculine as any poet's in the world. So he speaks of taking that same moon "from a crate of crooked trees," and he gives a gigantic suggestion of sinister strength in a few simple lines describing the windy Pacific Ocean:

> The shattered water made a misty din.
> Great waves looked over others coming in,
> And thought of doing something to the shore

8

That water never did to land before.
The clouds were low and hairy in the skies,
Like locks blown forward in the gleam of eyes.
You could not tell, and yet it looked as if
The shore was lucky in being backed by cliff,
The cliff in being backed by continent;
It looked as if a night of dark intent
Was coming, and not only a night, an age.
Someone had better be prepared for rage.
There would be more than ocean-water broken
Before God's last *Put out the Light* was spoken.

No one can say this poet has not looked immensity in
the face, who has written,

Great waves looked over others coming in.

Frost is as sparing in his use of figures of speech as
any poet we have had in English literature. He is afraid
of figures as he is afraid of symbols. Yet he believes in
them. He believes in great ones, the ones that grow naturally out of the organism of a poem. He believes in figures
that are inevitable and structural and alive. Frost men-
tions, in his *Education by Poetry*—one of his talks that
got taken down by a stenographer without his knowing
it—a metaphor he admires in the *Odyssey*. It is that one
which represents the shipwrecked and exhausted Odysseus
covering himself over with leaves, as people cover over
their seeds of fire on the hearth at night. Frost likes that
figure. Frost likes to think of a man's being thought of
as seeds of fire. Frost admires that metaphor because it
works the way his own mind works.

In the whole range of the literature that I am acquainted

with, I have three favorite figures of speech. The first
one is two thousand years old. A man whose head is full
of founding a city of his own comes upon a sight that
warms his heart. He sees a strange, great city being built;
work is humming, the walls swarm with busy men. The
whole scene glows with hot activity. And the man who
is looking at Carthage building sees it as a vast beehive.
The poet, there, is Virgil. His figure of speech is a right
one. He knew bees, and he knew great building, for he
had a great part in building the grandeur that was the
Roman Empire. Ever since I read that description as a
boy, I have connected bees with heat and with the Romans.
I think both are hot things, and they certainly belong
together. . . . You have to come more than a thousand
years our way to find my next favorite figure of speech.
A man who loves the earth is in a new kind of earth, a
gray one, where everything is indistinct. It is a place filled
with people who are dead to the old world, but still pur-
suing the course of man on another level of being. They
go around in their dusky world peering the way people
do back on earth in the dusking time, under the new
moon. The poet, this time, is Dante. He knew about this
world and about twilight and keen and eager people; and
he knew about two other worlds that only medieval men
could know about exactly. The figure of speech is a right
one. . . . And for my last, you will have to come forward again six hundred years, and you will have to come
to a farmhouse such as I used to live in, in New England.
You will have to come round by the kitchen door, where
the morning-glories grow on twine strings. It is twilight

again, as in Dante's poem, but we are still on the earth, this time, the homely, familiar earth. A plain farmer and his wife are sitting on their back-doorstep. They are talking about a broken-down hired man, who used to work for them and who has now come back. He is inside the house. They do not know it as yet, but he is dead. The farmer is pretty sure he has no hankering to have the man back. His wife thinks they might take him in. As she talks, the woman puts out her hand into the one spot of beauty she has on the farm, her flower-bed by the doorstep,

> Among the harp-like morning-glory strings,
> Taut with the dew from garden bed to eaves,
> As if she played unheard some tenderness
> That wrought on him beside her in the night.

That is a good figure of speech. It is the only one in a fairly long poem. It is a poem of plain speaking about plain people. The figure stands out all the more for being just that one touch of tenderness. A New England housewife playing on the only harp she will ever have, a harp with wires of twine string. But on these strings are the notes of blue morning-glories. The poet who wrote that figure of speech knows about morning-glory vines and hired men and the codes of New England. He knows about simple, honest people. And his knowledge has room for love. The man is Robert Frost. I know that all three of these are good figures of speech. For they all come right out of life. And they make me feel, in spite of the trouble and sadness always in the world, very glad to be alive.

V

A WIDER PATTERN OF SYMPATHY

One of the best signs of our times, I think, is the widening of the pattern of poetry. Now I admit the narrowness in several of our poets. We have some poets who make a cult of the unusual and turn in upon themselves to find sins that are unique and virtues that want a name. We have other poets, like Jeffers, who see life as a disease for which there is no cure save utter annihilation resembling that on the dead hills of the moon. We have poets who would make poetry a foreign language to all save the elected few. And yet we have poets, perhaps never so many before as now, who, in spite of the disintegration of the old ideas about religion and society, find more and more to believe in. And these poets—Lindsay was one, and Carl Sandburg is another—are orators, as the old poets used to be. Not that they use the old words or the old charters of belief. They have new gospels in the new tongue. But they are orators in that they try to convince people that life is worth living. They preach poetry. They have experienced something that has made them proud men and filled them with eagerness to live, and they want to share that experience with as many men as they can. They want a greater and greater audience. That is why both these poets have taken to the road as revivalists. They have taken to the roads where men gather most. For the sake of converts, they are ready and willing to snatch up into their orations the language and oral poetry that are common to the commonest people. They burn to be understood. And they will speak the people's tongue. They have taken upon themselves even the faults of the people, the thoughtless exuberance and the love of the sensational. For they have a precious thing to say, and they will sacrifice much to say it. It is a conviction of the goodness of man. Modern science has done a great deal in tabulating the deficiencies of man; astronomy has measured him against remoter space, psychology against his animal instincts, chemistry has measured him against materials of which his body and brain are composed. But Lindsay and Sandburg will still stand up and shout of man's worth.

Robert Frost desires a wide audience, too. He is an orator, and he has a conviction that his experience of poetry can be of some benefit to others. He is not a preacher. He is not a revivalist. He will not go more than his half of the road to make friends with people through his poetry. He will go his half way, though, and he has many friends. His ability to make so many friends is, I believe, a sign of great strength. Poetry belongs to the people. It does not belong to the poets, surely. That is one fact that Mr. Eliot and Mr. Pound have forgotten, among many, in their private service of song. Poetry does not belong to the scholars. When Robert Frost was giving the Norton Lectures at Harvard two years ago, he spoke to a crowded lecture hall every time he spoke. One day, somebody commented upon the fact that there had been some soldiers, even, in Mr. Frost's audience. Why not? I know of no people who need poetry more than soldiers. I speak from experience, having been a soldier for two years, myself. I should like to submit Mr. Eliot's poems to an audience of soldiers. It is true that Frost's audiences are catholic ones, as well as large ones.

Frost likes audiences. He likes to talk. He likes to read his poems, but he likes to talk about poetry in between. He doesn't like to talk just for the sake of talking, as some orators have been known to do. He has something to say. He has something to do each time he gets up to speak. It is a rather wonderful thing. It is not just the exposition of the process of poetry. It is the process itself. It is something very much alive. Frost has been making poems out of talk all his life, and now he is making talk itself the beginnings of poems. The Greeks had a word for poetry. They had the words for so many things! It was the verb *make*. They named the poet after what he did. And his product, too. *The maker made a making.* The accent, you see, is on the action. Well, Robert Frost, when he rises and talks, is like that Greek idea. He is *poetry in action.* I mean this. You can watch him *create.* You can hear his brain work. And, if you are near enough to him, you can see it. For Frost's face is one of the kind that can light up from inside. It is an extraordinary thing to hear a brain work the way a poet's does. It is a good sight to see light created. That is what poetry is, the sudden lighting up of a mind. It is like seeing a new chicken come out of its shell. By the way, the Royal Society of England began by watching chickens come out of the shell. You may think you know what to expect, but you are always surprised. You are always surprised

at the newness of a good poem on an old theme. Many
of the best ones are old. When you see and hear Robert
Frost talking about poetry, you are catching a poet in the
act. You are hearing some of the best poems that he is
going to put down in written words, later. It was a great
experience to hear Vachel Lindsay reciting his poems. I
heard him first at Oxford, in those halls of agony, the
Examination Schools. Some of the Oxford dons had come,
I feel sure, to scoff. They remained to pray—or at least
sing. I heard them joining in on the choruses. For Lindsay was able to go back and write his poems over by
living them over in his voice. In Frost's case, you get in
back of the poem, even, before it has taken the final form,
when it is beginning and growing and changing shape,
when it is just coming. This is one of the revelations of
our time, hearing Frost talk. It is more important than
reading some of the most expert of all the modern
treatises on the poetic art. It is poetry in the making.

Frost has many different titles to his talks. *Does Wisdom Matter?* That was one of the Harvard ones. Another
is *Opposites.* Still another is *Neither or Both.* And for
another, *Crudities.* But they are all very much alike in
showing the astounding integrity and clearness and confidence of this poet. For another thing, Frost often repeats
his talks. Yet they are a new thing each time. They may
be the beginnings of different poems. He does not remember just what things he said on the topic last time. "I may
be able to bring some of them back in detail," he writes,
"give me time. What in the world did I say in New
York? . . . Do you want to show me the notes you

made?" Frost did not have any notes, himself. He was talking about a poem that might happen later on. It does not matter what his subject is, you hear words that are alive, and they are joining themselves together to make a larger living tissue. They are as much a part of Frost as his poems are. They are the soil from which his poems spring. You hear him experimenting, turning his ideas over to see what he will find.

Another interesting thing: Frost does not write his talks down. So principles that might stiffen in their joints and become philosophies remain rules of thumb, horse-sense, that fairly rare thing, human wisdom. Frost has a fear of the abstract; he likes images and objects. Frost wants to remain a talker, he does not aspire to be a philosopher. The one requires an audience, the other does not. A talker, who is a poet, needs to use wit and humor and sympathy, the other can do without them. Frost does not like to write his talks down even after he has given them. That would mean they would "set," as he puts it. It would mean the end of that act of creating, the end of so many poems that might spring out of the talk. Written down, his talks would become finished and what Frost terms a part of his "literary" life: "I'm terrible about my lectures," he tells me in a letter. "In my anxiety to keep them as long as possible from becoming part of my literary life, I leave them rolling round in my head like clouds rolling round in the sky. Watch them long enough and you'll see one near-form change into another near-form." The figure of the cloud here is a remarkably apt and striking illustration of what happens when Frost talks. If you recall your high white thunderclouds, you will remember what a magnificent sight it is to see them grow. Frost's ideas, in talk, are like those restless shapes of lovely life. Frost goes on in his letter about his talks: "Though I am sure they are hardly permissible on the platform, I continue to bring them there with no more apology than to a parlor or class room. Their chief value to me is for what I pick up from them when I cut across them with a poem under emotion. They have been my inner world of raw material and my instinct has been to keep them raw. That can't long remain their state however. The day approaches when they will lose their fluidity and in spite of my stirring spoon become crystal. Then one kind of fun will be over and I shall have to find another to take its place (tennis most likely or hoeing). I thought I was about ready to let them set when I accepted the Harvard invitation to deliver them in writing after delivering them by word of mouth. Something in me still fights off the written prose. The nearest I ever came to getting myself down in prose was in the preface to Robinson's *King Jasper*." A photograph of a thundercloud is not the living thing the cloud is.

I can share this feeling of Frost's because I have already discovered, in a modest way for myself, that a poet can plan his future poems and feel them take shape inside himself while he talks about poetry. It is an experience that is about as satisfying as any joy a human being can know, I think. I have resisted the demands of the news people to send even a brief of my talks. Once I was caught out, for there was a court stenographer present

when I spoke, and he got down what I said. He spoiled
a number of future poems for me! Frost writes me that
he had the same experience. A smuggled-in stenographer
got him down in that article, *Education by Poetry*, I have
been quoting in these lectures. I suspected as much, for
the article reads like talk.

And one final comment on Frost's talking. And here
again I can join him in his experience through experience
of my own. There is in such talking to people and arousing their sympathy something very reassuring to one's
sense of the importance of poetry. To see an audience become excited, as you become excited, to see the audience
anticipate you and leap to your conclusions before you
reach them—this is to experience poetry. This can teach
creation in you. The sympathy Frost creates is a very sure
evidence that his ideas on poetry are very much alive.
This is the new *Ars Poetica*. It is poetry in community,
and it makes the whole country partners of a poet.

There is need of arousing such sympathy in the world
just now. It is essential that poets should convince people
of the goodness of new patterns in living, when so many
old ones are going or gone. In religion, in governments,
in economics, in the structure of society, even in learning
itself, so many of the things our fathers lived by are
crumbling that their very gospels may soon need trans-
lating to us even though they are written in our tongue,
and our fathers' very epitaphs may become a foreign language to their sons. When laws and languages fail, poets
must step in and create new. For it is to them the nations
have always looked for designs in living. Poets must

teach men to admire and worship life anew. They cannot be jaded or tired men. Of all alive, they must be the most intent on living.

Edwin Arlington Robinson poses the new questions that poets now are called upon to answer. If they do not answer, who will? The world seems to be changing, the refinements and nobilities of the past are broken and discarded. The poet must find the *whys* and *wherefores*. Robinson sought them earnestly all his life. You can hear agony in his quiet questioning in *King Jasper:*

> No God,
> No Law, no Purpose, could have hatched for sport
> Out of warm water and slime, a war for life
> That was unnecessary, and far better
> Never had been—if man, as we behold him,
> Is all it means.

Robinson could not find the major answers. But he found some of the second magnitude. He found that men can still put trust in man's endurance, even now when the subconscious has woven vast new universes of doom to overawe and annihilate him, in man's doing his lonely best—for the good man is always alone in spite of wife and children and friends—and not running away. There is room in the world still for courage and mercy, and, best of all, great pity, as that of Jasper for his wife as he hears her feet going out of his life. It is a reaffirmation of man's sturdy heroism against great odds. The common creator of kings and queens, Shakespeare, stands up and earns only a good living when his mind is living on the level of the gods. The average man from Stratford can

never know, in any age, what tragedies and what universes of hungry space make up the heart of a poet. The
man in the street can never guess how hard it is for a
poet to love mankind and never be able to lift a hand to
help men.—These are the negative eloquences of Robinson. But there can be even a great poetry of failure, if
it is the poetry of one like Robinson who "resolutely
leans towards the directness, simplicity, sanity and order,
which in his mind are the only forms suited to sincere
observation of facts, a clear-sighted understanding of
character, a balanced interpretation of conduct and a
vigorous insight into the permanent truths of life." That
is how Charles Cestre, the great French critic of a great
American mind, has summed up Robinson's answers of
the second magnitude. There is nobility to a man who
tries so hard and so humanly to answer all the questions
and yet is never able to do that, but only to go down like
a silent figure against the western sky and leave the
greatest question of all unanswered.

Robinson poses the questions. But Frost finds answers
to the questions. He finds them in a new awareness to
nature and human nature, in local loveliness, in a fresh
wonder at the world. He finds the answers in a new testament of neighborliness, in the kinship of men. He turns
his back on the intellectual absolutes, and finds a new
kind of absolute in the art of being a common human
being. He finds absolutes in slight things: a crow's wing
shakes snow down on him from a limb; and that makes
up for a lost day. He responds to life in a hundred new
objects the older poets passed by. He stretches out his

sympathy to include many neglected designs. To list the new subjects of this poet is to prove that the pattern of poetry has widened immensely since Tennyson's day: tramps on muddy country roads, a woodchuck, roadside stands, old shoes, a woodpile, a gum-gatherer, a line-gang, a census-taker, a kitchen chimney, brush for peas, a man's slide with a lantern, and against his wishes, down a mountain on an icy night—all these are poems to Frost, because these are parts of life, and parts of life are poetry as much as the whole. Some of these parts are humorous, but when was that ever anything against their being poetic? The poetic is the close observation of the fine articulations of creation. You can see these articulations of creation in a man the worse for wear, sitting shrewdly down in a snowdrift and planning his way home, just as surely as you can see them in a man doing something on a state occasion. The articulations are there, in both cases. Here is the drunken man in the snowdrift, in *Willful Homing*, a recent poem:

> It is growing dark and time he drew to a house
> But the blizzard blinds him to any light ahead.
> The snow gets down his neck in a chilly souse
> That sucks his breath like a wicked cat in bed.
>
> The snow blows on him and off him exerting force
> Downward to make him sit astride a drift,
> Imprint a saddle and calmly consider his course.
> He peers out shrewdly into the thick and swift.
>
> Since he means to come to a door he will come to a door,
> Although so compromised of aim and rate.
> He may fumble wide of the latch a yard or more
> And to those concerned he may seem a little late.

There is no reservation for the poetic. It is found in the small places as well as the large.

And all this local loveliness of law is for Frost a sign that a kind of universal law is running the universe still. The joy in multitudinous small objects can be expanded to fill the universe—and science just at the moment informs us that the universe *is* expanding—in spite of all the disasters that threaten men now. God may seem very far away at times in Frost, and this man invokes his name very sparingly and gently, as becomes a New Englander, but the chances are God is still somewhere on hand. Maybe one trouble in the past was we got to depending on him for too much. If God isn't there every time a man inquires for him, it may well be the man isn't more than half there himself.

> I turned to speak to God
> About the world's despair;
> But to make bad matters worse
> I found God wasn't there.
>
> God turned to speak to me
> (Don't anybody laugh)
> God found I wasn't there—
> At least not over half.

Men ought to have more confidence in the good—or God, if you want to call it that—now when men have to lean on themselves and one another more. This is a revolutionary idea and something of fresh wonder in poetry, to think it may do us good to do without God more and find more of him in ourselves. Homely companionship, as Frost describes it, is not without its light of glory. So a walk Frost took by night with his English friend, on the old Malvern Hills where William Langland saw heaven six hundred years ago, turns into a walk surrounded by an aureole. The moon started it, it made a rainbow over the two men. But then the rainbow

> lifted from its dewy pediment
> Its two mote-swimming many-colored ends,
> And gathered them together in a ring.
> And we stood in it softly circled round
> From all division time or foe can bring
> In a relation of elected friends.

Here is another kind of homecoming from that of the man drunkenly straddling the snowdrift. It is good that men can come home with haloes round their heads, too. Mysterious earth-light and the mysterious light of friendship can wall men round against all the disasters and doubts the years can bring. Frost and his friend coming down Malvern Hill are the answer to the lonely figure Robinson saw going down his hill surrounded in the sunset with questions no man can find the answer to. Frost is shy of symbols. But the symbols he is shy of are the ones that poets invent. When symbols come naturally in nature, he is glad to set them down and make a poem of them, as he does here in *Iris by Night*. Science has pushed the stars far away from the world and made them seem careless and cruel. They don't seem to be so worried about our nativities as they used to be in the Middle-Age time. They don't stir our lives up any more in love and war. But Frost trusts in the designs of man and doesn't worry about "otherworldliness."

We may as well go patiently on with our life
And look elsewhere than to stars and moon and sun
For the shocks and changes we need to keep us sane.

We can do without the old stars. There are enough new ones in ourselves. Frost has a sense of the destiny of the human race. It isn't an elaborated schedule of improvements that the older New England poets subscribed to. We aren't due at the millenium, or any way-station this side of it, at such and such a time. But we are getting on. We are getting on because we are learning to get on better with one another. And the most remarkable thing is that our destiny seems to be in the right direction, the direction of happiness. This wasn't true of some of the destinies we have had in the world before now. This is a widening of the poetic pattern, for sure. This amounts to a new doctrine of man.

Man?—It is wider than that. Man used to be men's central concern when poets wrote, and no longer ago than when our grandfathers were young and could go and hear Mr. Emerson preach in Boston. In the Middle Ages, of course, man was the jewel hung on the middle of the chain of God's creatures. He had the place of honor. Maybe the older poets thought too much about that place of honor, that jewel of honor, and forgot about the links of the chain, the other creatures. That is not so now. For poets everywhere, in every tongue I know of, are beginning to make a remarkable discovery of the honor and rightness in what our fathers used to call the brute creation. Animals and birds and fish, and even beetles and the slower creatures, the trees and stones, are coming into

9

poetry as never before. They are coming in, not as lower forms of life, but as members of a vast brotherhood of all that is and grows, all that swims and crawls and flies, and all that is marked for death early or late. It is a new sympathy that goes into the cool earth and into the cold places of the sea and finds doomed and marvelously intricate loveliness there. Elinor Wylie writes of the sadness in the eyes of toads and fishes. Men have opened their eyes to the beauty of the adder, "a flowing jewel in the brake," and to the "luminous breath of fireflies." These are remarkable articulations of life the older poets mostly passed by, or used only as the margins to man. Now they have come into poetry in their own right. Their numbers are legion; there are as many new poems possible as there are kinds of creatures that fly or run. And man has put himself into their bodies and feels with them, as Lew Sarett feels with the four baby foxes, blue with the cold of March, as they whimper and nuzzle one another, now that their mother is slain and does not come home. This is not a case of man's condescending to lean and stroke the animals. The poet has not gone down. He has raised the earth in his hands to the level of his heart. He has put his arms around the trees and the rocks and the deer pursued by hounds. It is an enlargement of life, clearly. It is a hymn of universal brotherhood we are hearing on every side, a hymn of all men and all forms of life. It is the new song of honor:

> The everlasting pipe and flute
> Of wind and sea and bird and brute,
> And lips deaf men imagine mute
> In wood and stone and clay,

The music of a lion strong
That shakes a hill a whole night long,
A hill as loud as he,
The twitter of a mouse among
Melodious greenery,
The ruby's and the rainbow's song,
The nightingale's—all three,
The song of life that wells and flows
From every leopard, lark and rose
And everything that gleams or goes
Lack-lustre in the sea.

I heard it all, each, every note
Of every lung and tongue and throat,
Ay, every rhythm and rhyme
Of everything that lives and loves
And upward, ever upward moves
From lowly to sublime!
Earth's multitudinous Sons of Light,
I heard them lift their lyric might
With each and every chanting sprite
That lit the sky that wondrous night
As far as eye could climb!

I heard it all, I heard the whole
Harmonious hymn of being roll
Up through the chapel of my soul
And at the altar die,
And in the awful quiet then
Myself I heard, Amen, Amen,
Amen I heard me cry!
I heard it all and then although
I caught my flying senses, Oh,
A dizzy man was I!
I stood and stared; the sky was lit,
The sky was stars all over it,

I stood, I knew not why,
Without a wish, without a will,
I stood upon that silent hill
And stared into the sky until
My eyes were blind with stars, and still
I stared into the sky.

It is interesting to read T. S. Eliot's cynical comments on Ralph Hodgson, who wrote these lines. I know what the cynical may say of this multiplication of the themes of poetry to include new forms of existence. He may say it is fruit of degradation growing out of the doctrines of Darwin and Huxley. Man has been degraded to the brute, and so he will grovel and sing with his kind. Man fallen so low will sing of the low. But this is not the case. It may be the theory of evolution has opened the way for this new poetry. But it is an elevation of life, not a degradation of it, and the creatures and man rise together in their brotherhood, to new designs of swiftness and strength, splendor and tenderness. The song is an honorable one. It is full of admiration and love.

The New England poet, Robert Frost, has his voice in this new and vast song of honor. He sings his part in his own way, but his part fits into the grand, new whole. Frost sings his stanzas with less magnificence than Ralph Hodgson, but with no less heartiness. He subscribes to the gospel of the brotherhood of creatures unobtrusively, gently, as he subscribes to God. He avoids the apocalyptic, he uses the tender and whimsical and humorous touch. But the belief in brotherhood is there. It is in his lines on the fine pullet that won a blue ribbon at Amesbury, lingering proudly over her meal and going last to roost. It is in the drumlin woodchuck that sits serenely at his front door, conscious of his back way out, and shrewdly pretends that he and the world are friends to each other. This isn't merely a woodchuck's moral, of course, it is one for the whole human race. The wasp is part of Frost's quiet song of brothers, an egoist "on glossy wires artistically bent," who thinks he is "as good as anybody going." And the white-tailed hornet comes in, too, for his part. He lives in a balloon, made out of Japanese crêpe-paper, hanging in the woodshed, with a door like the mouth of a gun pointed in the direction of business. He comes out of that door better than a bullet, for he can always change direction in flight, and stings the man who visits him. But when he visits with the man, in the man's house, it is different:

> As visitor at my house he is better.
> Hawking for flies about the kitchen door,
> In at one door perhaps and out another,
> Trust him then not to put you in the wrong.
> He won't misunderstand your freest movements.
> Let him light on your skin unless you mind
> So many prickly grappling feet at once.
> He's after the domesticated fly
> To feed his thumping grubs as big as he is.
> Here he is at his best, but even here—
> I watched him where he swooped, he pounced, he struck;
> But what he found he had was just a nailhead.

This is an accurate description of a creature whose articulations are fine enough for anybody's poem. But it is more. That hornet's mistaking a nailhead for a fly is mighty revealing to Robert Frost. It brings to his mind the whole problem of the theory of evolution and the "downward comparisons," as Frost calls them, that followed. The assigning of instinct to animals and error to man. Frost thinks the whole business needs revision. As long as men made comparisons upward, they were only a little lower than the angels. Now "downward comparisons" have left men and animals both degraded. It is time for all hands to start up again, maybe, seeing that a hornet can make mistakes just as well as the man can. The right to make mistakes was about all the doctrine of evolution left as ours! We can't go any lower. So maybe we can all go up. Maybe the whole doctrine of descent was wrong. Maybe it should be a doctrine of ascent. All this can serve as an introduction to the new philosophy of sympathy. One of the loveliest instances of sympathy with the creatures is Frost's poem *On a Bird Singing in Its Sleep.* To suppose that a poet so in love with common idioms of speech and the common object and mind is incapable of firm and delicate distinctions of pattern, is not to know Robert Frost. Here is a poem as full of ordered and intricate relationships as those in *Paradise Lost.* If it is of a bird, and not of a higher form such as an Adam or an angel of darkness or light, this study of beauty singing in the dark and obeying the laws of light is as moving as anything yet written to justify the ways of God to his creatures:

> A bird half wakened in the lunar noon
> Sang half way through its little inborn tune.
> Partly because it sang but once all night

And that from no especial bush's height;
Partly because it sang ventriloquist
And had the inspiration to desist
Almost before the prick of hostile ears,
It ventured less in peril than appears.
It could not have come down to us so far
Through the interstices of things ajar
On the long bead chain of repeated birth
To be a bird while we are men on earth
If singing out of sleep and dream that way
Had made it much more easily a prey.

Concern for the small lives of sparrows and the lilies of the field is an element of Scripture. It is only lately that our poets have begun to make it a major theme in poetry, and so open up whole continents to the art. This is no reading into creatures men's yearning and wistfulness. These creatures in the new poetry are seen in their authentic form, as no camera can see them. They are hot wasps working their "stinging quarters" realistically. It is a sparrow-hawk, with eyes set on opposite sides of his head, seeing

the circle of the world
Alive with wings that he was born
To rend.

This is a reading out from the creatures a poetry of successful competition with chaos and death just as important as man's competition with the same enemies. It is something as new as this year's nestling. It is a new testament of the "togetherness" of all created life. These young horses are colts, and they feel in their four feet and a tail. But what they feel about the dark and the storm is what a child would feel; they are our kin on the edge of the formless unknown. So these young horses must be comforted in the universal language all mothers will use, whether they go on four feet or two. It is only accidental, too, that this mother's talk is in the New England idiom:

The Runaway

Once when the snow of the year was beginning to fall,
We stopped by a mountain pasture to say, "Whose colt?"
A little Morgan had one forefoot on the wall,
The other curled at his breast. He dipped his head
And snorted at us. And then he had to bolt.
We heard the miniature thunder where he fled,
And we saw him, or thought we saw him, dim and grey,
Like a shadow against the curtain of falling flakes.
"I think the little fellow's afraid of the snow.
He isn't winter-broken. It isn't play
With the little fellow at all. He's running away.
I doubt if even his mother could tell him, 'Sakes,
It's only weather.' He'd think she didn't know!
Where is his mother? He can't be out alone."
And now he comes again with clatter of stone,
And mounts the wall again with whited eyes
And all his tail that isn't hair up straight.
He shudders his coat as if to throw off flies.
"Whoever it is that leaves him out so late,
When other creatures have gone to stall and bin,
Ought to be told to come and take him in."

Here in one of Frost's poems that he loves best to read because they are his best, the hymn of the sympathy of all the created is heard at its simplest best. The poem is all the more eloquent for the place of its origin. This is a

New England pattern of chaos, a New England snowstorm, and this is a Morgan colt, a tough, small son of the
New England grass and will-to-live. He is closer to human children, maybe, because he is more a member of
the family than other horses, say, on a Kentucky stock
farm. New Englanders have always made more of their
animals than other people because they have fewer of
them, and because they have had to guard them more
against the weather. New England barns are a part of
the house; they are joined to the house by a series of
rooms. But they are a part of the house in more than
mere carpentry. They always have been, for the Small-
House New Englander, the other parlor, the other best
room of the house. More living has gone on in them than
in the front parlor. More living by the hour and by the
day, more living by the month and the year and by the
lifetime. It is a room of friends of the family, four-
footed and feathered, kin of the family, really. I have
found some of my best poems in barns. A barn is the best
place to go to find a poem ready-made. Here is a poem
of mine from that other best room of the New England
house:

Winter Milking

Five o'clock, and snow knee-deep,
More in the air before men sleep.
The night is thick a foot behind,
A foot before, I stumble blind
With too much light in one small space,
I lower the lantern from my face.
Now I am in, and shut the door,
Stamp the snow off on the floor,

Set the lantern by the sill.
The tie-up suddenly grows so still
I hear a squeaky mouse in the bin,
Vast, sweet breaths are taken in
Behind the door. I dole out grain,
And now the breaths rush out again,
Stanchions rattle, bodies stir;
I open the door on minever,
Velvet, sunshine in sleek hair,
And honey and clover in the air.
Round eyes burn on me, tongues caress
Blue nostrils wide with eagerness.
I put the feed-boxes in place,
Hunger furnishes the grace.

I take my stool and pail and sit
Under a cow and stroke the teat
With fingers in sequence down the five,
I feel her milk come down alive,
Tinkling stream, then thick and thicker,
Between my knees ascends the liquor
Until the warmth of it goes deep
Into my thigh bones as I keep
The pail in place. I lean my head
Against her flank above me spread.
I feel my blood and hers as one,
Full of contentment and of sun.
Over the ridgepole whirls new snow,
And I bow my head and know
That for this moment we are kin,
This creature I have taken in
And I whose kind rose so above
The roots of earth we missed such love
As I feel now upon my brow
Pressed to the velvet of a cow.
Under the thousand miles of night

I sit in a tiny world of light,
And shapes of unknown woe and death
Go over me in the sobbing breath
Of the storm outside, but I sit calm
With love on my forehead like a palm.

I am especially proud of this poem because it made me a fine friend, Mrs. Sidney Lanier, the wife of the great Baltimore poet Lanier's son. She read my poem and decided she wanted to know me, and she went about doing it, I am glad to say. I think this poem is a small instance of the great promise in this poetry of the brotherhood of creatures. I think that we have had that poetry being written for many years now, in the form of living, in the small houses and big barns of northern New England. And now our poets are beginning to collect it, and put it into books. Such poetry is endless, it seems to me. I have written dozens of poems of these meetings of animals and men on an equal footing; and I have only begun to stir the ground. Other poems are there. And they are fresh and new and fill a man with wonder and make him glad to be alive and a part of a living poetry wide as the world.

It would be a man wilfully blind who could not see behind and above all this new sense of kinship among all the living a pattern of poetry—perhaps the finest pattern of all poetry—which is as old as the race and the oldest religions, and yet is always new. That is the pattern we give the name *mysticism* to. The word is a technical one, and it is easy to give it a technical interpretation that will confuse and sometimes confound the greatest scholars of poetry. But really the word stands for a very simple and single truth, and a comforting truth: the oneness of being. All the pieces of life belong together; the daisy is blood-brother of Aldebaran; red blood and the diamond-colored blood of ants and angels are the same brave fluid that works out rhythms to confound dead and empty space. The lovely dance of life in electrons is just as much in the fountain which is the sap rising in a February tree as in the great surf the nebulae throw up on the distant outer beaches of the universe. They all make up a one out of a myriad. A one with a face and a will to overcome darkness and disintegration. Call the one Providence or Plan, or Zeus or God, it does not matter; the one is there. And between the parts of the whole are what Shakespeare has called "understood relations." It takes a poet to see them. Robert Frost sees them. He sees them between a maple tree and a child named after the tree; and the child grew into a woman whose whole life was arranged for her by a secret sympathy her mother had felt just on her way out of life, when she and her baby met for one brief sight. The father did not know what that poem name had meant.

> But it seems like some word she left to bid you
> Be a good girl—be like a maple tree.

And so a life of right design began. There is this sense of prearranged pattern in things back of Frost's poems. It is all the more telling because it is implied, and is like an overtone about his words, lingering after his poem is done. It is second nature with this poet, not second sight.

It depends on no earthquakes or sudden rending of the sky. The light comes through with the light of common day. But it is a far light and a clear light, and it makes life seem better than the sum of its parts. Without the necessity of fear of the hereafter or any hint of damnation, without a hierarchy of deity, this mysticism amounts to a natural good feeling about creation. It is a light of understanding that puts a nimbus, not on Sunday, but on daily, bread. A man can go far by that light. He can go far to being kind and observant and alive to the wonder everywhere around him. Frost shares in this more natural manifestation of the mystical than poetry has ever known before. It is a mysticism more moving, it seems to me, than Whitman's or Emerson's. It is more like Sidney Lanier's and Emily Dickinson's kind. Whatever it is, it is one of the finest things alive on our planet today. And Frost's quiet use of it is one more proof that what begins as sectional and New England poetry can end by being poetry wide enough to cover the world.

VI

A NEW KIND OF SALVATION

Every poet who is an orator and not merely an explorer of private woes and pleasures ought to set up some sort of guideposts to help humanity along the way. He ought to give some very specific advice about living. I say this, in spite of the fact that modern times are being very hard on guideposts and almost every form of *haec fabula docet*. People today want to take their art and their morals, whatever ones they may have, separately. But great poetry never lays itself open to the attack of little critics, whatever age it happens in. It is only the poetry of the second magnitude, such as much of that in the middle of the nineteenth century, that goes into battle with an Achilles tendon of morality exposed. Robert Frost and Edwin Arlington Robinson are great enough poets to hide the law under the form of life. And both men teach life. That is their reason for writing.

It is hard to call this help these poets render philosophy. That is too high and hard a word to do for either. All through these lectures, I have had to avoid the absolute in words as I have had to avoid the absolute in ideas. Philosophy is not the right name; for philosophy has always been a kind of *ignis fatuus* for poets. It has led them away from life; higher than life, if you will, but away. And I believe that even the philosophical poets, Lucretius and Dante and Goethe, have succeeded in being

126

great poets because, however far above or below life philosophy may have led them, they have kept the color of humanity and the color of the leaves and dawn and evening in their words. Lucretius is most moving when he sings of the manifestations of light and sound in small earthy creatures; and Dante is at his best in hell, where the most interesting people are. Philosophy leads away from life. But the direction of Robinson and Frost is towards life. They run always into the midst of it. Robinson, though he writes always with a sense of detachment, does not teach detachment. And Robert Frost preaches— as much as any good Monday and Tuesday talker can preach anything—attachment for all the minutes a man is awake. He is so attached to things that he reminds one of his own apple gatherer who keeps the shape of the ladder rung on his instep and the sound of apples rolling into the cellar all through his hours of rest and deep into his sleep. He thinks thoughts that take him high and low, but he always keeps the shape of objects in his eyes and his hands.

Yet these men teach a kind of gospel, for all their attachment to the concrete. Gospel is too big a word. It implies too much, it implies the idea of reform. But there must be some word for their system of encouragement of mankind. For it is a system, and they do encourage. Testament is the nearest, maybe, we can come to it. New Testament, because it grows out of a new set of years and needs. Testament seems a good term, for these poets teach by example. They leave their experience of life as their moral. They testify by action; Frost by his own catholic activity as much as anything, Robinson by the actions of the men and women he has made to act his life for him. They preach or teach by experience. If I know how to read my *Bible*, this is the difference between the Old and New Testaments: the Old teaches by revelation from on high, the New by the daily actions of men who have experienced the light. I know I run a great risk in our generation by constantly using terms from the *Bible*. But I must run that risk because, as so often happens in life, the *Bible* has the best words for literature as well as ethics.

These poets teach salvation. That, too, is an apocalyptic word such as Frost would go around several White or Green mountains to avoid. But it is a word capable of meaning what Mary Magdalene found and Nicodemus found, as well as what John, the scribe, experienced on the island of Patmos, when one of the green little places dedicated to Aphrodite and Bacchus saw a hole ripped in the sky and sights to scare Bacchus and Aphrodite out of the world forever. Salvation, in the milder connotation, will have to do. Happiness won't do. For if modern living has taught us correctly, happiness is, like space and Euclid and his straight line, only a relative term. And, besides, happiness would be too small a word for the state of the times. Salvation is the only word that will do. It is a set of rules of thumb which Frost leaves us in his poems, and even more in his talks. So let me call his kind of salvation rule-of-thumb salvation. Frost leaves the mark of his thumb on most things he handles. And like Chaucer's miller, he has a thumb of gold. That is, his material has colored his being, and not the other way around. And since these rules for living come out more in his talking about poetry than in his poetry itself, I shall be speaking mostly about Frost's oral and prose poems today.

We have a special need of salvation today, whether the rule-of-thumb kind or the rule-of-intellect kind such as Robinson has so desperately and earnestly tried to find and has not wholly succeeded in doing so. For poetry, like other art forms, is being called upon to take the place of many mighty ancient things that are crumbling fast under the vibrations of our heavy traffic in material goods and our rapid forms of going and coming between points and arriving very, very seldom. Religions, or a lot of the essential parts of older religions, are crumbling, for most people, inside the oldest Christian church or out. Other edifices of belief are showing fissures, too; in the family, in marriage, in the education of the young, and in the forms of government. We are being shaken out of our old securities in time sense and space sense. New England, for instance, has grown smaller, apparently, and a day's ride will cover it all. A day's ride won't. In fact, it will pretty well miss everything of importance there. For instance, all the contours of the land are erased. But the illusion is disturbing enough to get put into textbooks and thought. Poetry is being called upon to assert once more the old truth that the more a number of things change, the more the few that matter remain the same. It is being called upon to maintain the old facts of courage and compassion and belief in life, in new terms. It is being called upon to do more: to erect a religion of

10

living to take the place of the religion that is lost. Some of the lost religion was a religion of dying, in any case. Perhaps we are passing through the process that the Greeks went through. It may be that poetry will have to take over religion, or such part of it as the vital myths, just as poetry took over the Greek mythical religion. One thing is sure, the art of poetry must become an art of life. Frost speaks of having lived with poetry all his years, as if it had hands and feet and a heart; and it is true that he has done that. Poetry was life itself for Robinson, too, the only life he had. It is not likely that we shall have aesthetics as a state religion, as the Greeks at their best had it; we are not the Greeks. But it is likely that we shall see a concept of poetry as a public function at least as wide as Milton's.

We must have belief, in any event. And poetry is an act of belief. Myth, it may be, at the start; make-believe is one kind of beginning for a poem. But make-believe must grow into faith. Men will never be able to argue faith out of the world as long as the arts are in it, and poetry will be the last of the arts to go because it is the one in which most people can share by direct representation and even by unconscious participation, as Frost has so often shown.

Among the talks of Robert Frost, there are a number that are small chapters in this poet's creed of belief in man. And I should like to examine several of these astoundingly keen and concrete criticisms of life—that is, of poetry, which is one and the same thing, with this man. I believe that these brief talks—" meditative monologues,"

Frost calls them—are among the most important pieces of literary criticism, and of life criticism, we have today, or have ever had. And I should like to relate them to Robinson's ideas wherever it is possible to do so.

For the first, there is Frost's meditation, *The Three Beliefs*. These beliefs are: self-belief, love-belief, and art or poetry-belief. "The person who gets close enough to poetry," Robert Frost declares, "he is going to know more about the word *belief* than anybody else knows, even in religion nowadays." It may be a myth, the very young man's assumption that he is something very important and new in the world. But the myth turns into the gospel truth if the young man believes in himself hard enough and long enough. He actually becomes that fine man he expected he was going to be. And the second belief is the love-belief. This seems to be an even more remarkable thing, for it concerns two separate universes. They have a foreknowledge of oneness, and if they get along happily together after they are united, that foreknowledge becomes actual knowledge. And the last of the three is the belief that is literary. "Every time a poem is written, every time a short story is written, it is written, not by cunning, but by belief. The beauty, the something, the little charm of the thing to be, is more felt than known." It is, as Frost represents it, a sort of an investment in the infinite. And it is a good work of art if you have invested right. And because each of these three beliefs is a form of investment in the infinite, they all tend to make a man come to believe in God. All kinds of believing are a partnership in God. I do not know that the reason for the existence of pride and love and poetry has ever been more effectively or more beautifully stated.

And how is it with Robinson here, in relation to this charter of salvation?—Well, he believed in self all through the years of neglect and the years of plenty, no man more. The second was not for him personally, but he believed in it for Tristram and the two Iseults almost as hard as the ancient narrators of the Tristram legend, although he had a thousand gnawing rats of modern psychology to stand off. Robinson believed in art, the third belief, above self and all things else. But he broke his heart all his life trying to bridge that chasm to a belief in God that Robert Frost finds as easy to cross as a sky-lit pool in the spring woods. This is the difference between the two poets, chiefly. But it is a difference that seems to make them poets almost of a different race.

The next oral meditation of Frost's I should like to take up is his theory of *Opposites*. I heard him give his talk on *Opposites* at the testimonial dinner given him by the Poetry Society of America, in New York City, on April 1st, 1937. It was a memorable end for any meal. The world at all times, he said, is full of opposites. He did not mean by these, qualities that are good and qualities that are bad. But qualities that are all so good that they destroy each other if they can. Conflicting goods, was what he meant. For instance, Justice is a good, and Mercy is its opposite; Being has the opposite of Becoming; Divine Right opposes Consent of the Governed; Humanness, Disinterestedness; Socialism, Individualism. In different times, one quality gets the upper hand; and then its opposite. The world is torn between extremes of the good. The wise man, and the good, tries to keep to the middle of the road, going his way in a third direction. He feels tugged at both sides, but he tries to walk a straight way to certainty. The poet, being such a wise man, has to "sway playfully and vitally" somewhere between these fierce and self-annihilating goods. This is a New England farmer-poet's conception of the Golden Mean, and it is one rooted, I think, in the long years of sober discipline New Englanders have undergone, not only in the spirit of independence in our town meetings and our weather, but also in our cautious desire to be fair. That desire shows itself in the habit of understatement. And it springs especially from the fact of limited resources. Where most people have had to be "saving" for many generations, the Golden Mean is like the Golden Rule. Frost illustrates his theory in a letter to me, using one of the homely illustrations for which his talks are so famous: "Justice and Mercy," says he, "stand each other off and the present stands up between them. . . . They are like the two hands that, by first tightening and then loosening the double string between them, make the tin buzzer buzz like a little buzz saw. You must have played," he adds, "with a tin buzzer on the Kennebeck." A choice of extremes was offered Robert Frost once, in a day when taste ran towards strong meat in literature as well as life:

"Prude, or puke,
Mewling and puking in the public arms."

Frost took the middle of the road:

> "Me for the hills where I don't have to choose."

It is clear, in all that Frost says and all that he writes, that he is of the party of Aristophanes, of the Center. He fears extremes, as all good older New Englanders fear extremes. He says he never dared to be radical while he was young, for fear he would have to be conservative when he got old. This big-hearted lover of common people has often, lately, aroused the ire of the professing proletarians. When one of these chided him with words out of Russia as a "counter-revolutionist," Frost countered by calling him a "bargain-counter-revolutionist." It is, I think, a good New England answer. Frost has good New England answers to the extremists in politics, the men who want everybody to sign up for whatever extreme creed is on the bandwagon at the moment. He calls them the "tendential" people. They are akin to the "tendential" critics who want Frost to climb on a radical or conservative bandwagon. "By tendential in politics," he says in a letter to me, "they mean what is sure to happen. After making sure it is going to happen, they don't trust it to happen of itself: they take hold and make it happen. Just so the horsey bets on a sure thing and then does all that in him lies with dope and counter dope, sponges in the nose, bribery and threat to make the sure thing surer. There is a horrid crudity of morals in our idealistic tendential friends." This is one of the best comments I have come across upon the fashionableness of revolution, whether on the right or left side of the road. If for no other reason, people will go red or black simply out of boredom. The thinkers are generally found in the unpopular middle of the road. And they generally receive all the missiles intended for either side. Frost goes on to say how "tendential" thinking produces most people's ideas: "Hegel saw two people marry and produce a third person. That was enough for Hegel—and Marx too, it seems. They jumped at the conclusion that so all truth was born. Out of two truths in collision today sprang the one truth to live by tomorrow. A time succession was the fallacy. Marriage, reproduction and the family with a big F have much to answer for in misleading the analogists. Fire flashes from the flint and steel of metaphor and if caught in lint it may be spread, but that is no reason why it should be spread to burn the world. That is monomania or monometaphor." Frost has very definite faith in nationalism, and even patriotism—which is a calf with a very different kink to his tail. He is old-fashioned enough to think that a man can begin being a good citizen of the world and a good internationalist by being a good citizen of his own country.

Poetry is an art of the Center. That center is not a dead center; it is anything but that. It is the most dangerous place to be, because it is the most unpopular place. "Life," Frost declares, "sways perilously at the confluence of opposing forces. Poetry in general plays perilously in the same wild place. In particular it plays perilously between truth and make-believe. It might be extravagant poetry to call it true make-believe—or making believe what is so."

Compromise is a New England virtue. And it is Robert Frost's. Compromise in New England and in Robert Frost is often making the best of things. The saving New England farmer begrudges every conical spruce on his pasture slope. But ambitious, sharp-eyed boys with axes are fine things, too, especially around Christmas time. And so the wise man, and the Christian, compromises and forgives the human good for destroying the green good. Here is a compromise Christmas card. It is called *To a Young Wretch,* and it is Frost's Christmas card of this last December:

I could have bought you just as good a tree
To frizzle resin in a candle flame;
And what a saving 'twould have been to me.
But tree by charity is not the same
As tree by enterprise and expedition.
I must not spoil your Christmas with contrition.

It is your Christmases against my woods,
But even where thus opposing interests kill,
They are to be thought of as conflicting goods
Oftener than as conflicting good and ill;
Which makes the war god seem no special dunce
For always fighting on both sides at once.

And though in tinsel chain and popcorn rope,
My tree, a captive in your window bay,
Has lost its footing on my mountain slope
And lost the stars of heaven, may oh may
The symbol star it lifts against your ceiling
Help me accept its fate with Christmas feeling.

And Edwin Arlington Robinson?—Although he was never the public spokesman for poetry that Frost is, he is of the party of the Center, too. He has the ability to see opposing goods, to see both sides of a question. He is fair with the Cavenders and the Zoës of the earth, the ones for whom love becomes too small and the ones for whom love grows too large. Robinson's greatest means to a kind of salvation is making the best of things, as Fargo makes the best of his disillusionment. But Robinson's compromise is full of shadow and sadness. He must compromise between men's apparent potentialities and their powers. He is courageous and charitable. But there is something of the sunset and resignation in his acceptance of life.

There is a third characteristic testament of talk by Robert Frost in which his New England contemporary has no share, maybe to his own hurt. For this talk is about things that have helped sharpen Frost's sense of humor and so keep him well. Frost calls this talk *Crudities*. It is about the raw and naïve manifestations of life which the Big-House New Englander hardly has room for in his conversations, but which may, for all that, as we shall see, come into them when he is regally unaware. Frost has an animus for the self-elected upholders of refinement. Such people I have found to be aptly described in the oral literature of New England as "nasty nice," or in the livery-stable metaphors, "high-steppers" and "head up and tail over the dashboard." Frost goes gunning for such people as the ones who are conscious of their cut-glass. He likes to begin with lower forms of crudity and get these people to laughing over these, and then go higher, until he makes them laugh at themselves. It is a study in a new humanism to see him carry out this plan at, say, a poetry club dinner. He likes to begin by telling about a neighbor he once had who was sure Ernest Poole was a better author than Frost was, because Poole's books cost him $1.50, and he could get Frost's book for $1.00. It was a New England rural neighbor, and the man had an eye to values. But it is only a step up to the next kind of crudity. Frost tells about a very interesting and traveled gentleman of business he met on a sleepless Pullman sleeper. They talked half the night, and the man did his best, politely, to discover what Frost's business was. Frost stalled him off and egged on his curiosity. He said he was an adventurer, like the business man; he was a "long-shot man" also, one who did not want to know what the next day might bring. "And so," Frost goes on, "till he lost patience with me and cried 'Shoot!' Well, I write poetry. 'Hell,' he said unhappily, 'my wife writes that stuff.' " So perished an adventurer in life! Frost sends me his latest adventure in crudity, in a letter that came by air mail, to be in time for these lectures: "A forty year old telegraph operatress had drawn her own inference from my telegrams. 'You write,' she said to me one day. Yes—'Poetry?' Yes. 'Just the person I'm looking for then. I lost my father a year or so ago and I'd like to get a poem written about him. I'll tell you what I want said.' She took paper and pencil." But how much worse, Frost asks, as he goes upstairs to the utterly refined people, is that telegraph "operatress" than a gentleman "out of Harvard, New York, real society and literature," who traveled a long way to ask Frost to save America by writing something American at last. The man was sure Frost could do it if he tried.

But this New England poet likes crudities, even in the highest places. He likes them in himself, for other people's sake, for poetry's sake. Crudity, when you come right down to it, is the very stuff of life. It is the soil from which the fragile and fine things spring. It is unshaped life. "I thank the Lord for crudity," Frost writes in a letter, "which is rawness, which is raw material, which is the part of life not yet worked up into form, or at least not worked all the way up. Meet with a fallacy of the foolish: having had a glimpse of finished art, they forever after pine for a life that shall be nothing but finished art. Why not a world safe for art," Frost asks, "as well as democracy? A real artist delights in roughness for what he can do to it. He's the brute who can knock the corners off the marble block and drag the unbedded beauty out of bed. The statesman (politician) is no different except he works in a protean mass of material that hardly holds the shape he gives it long enough for him to point it out and get credit for it. His material is the rolling mob. The poet's material is words that for all we may say and feel against them are more manageable than men. Get a few words alone in a study and with plenty of time on your hands you can make them say any thing you please."

There, by the way, is Frost at his best as a talker. Here is a sermon on life with right life in it everywhere, alive and kicking. "Drag the unbedded beauty out of bed"— his mind moves in metaphor every mother's son of us has had his hands on at one time or another. His words are solid things, and they strike out sparks as they hammer home at an idea. We can feel the heat of this man, talking talk that leads to a new testament of beauty.

It is largely out of Frost's raw material for art, the human crudities, the lovable manifestations of rough-handed living, that one of the greatest of the strengths of Robert Frost has sprung. This is his humor. A saving sense of humor is most certainly one of his best rule-of-thumb guides to salvation. For with this poet, laughing is a serious matter, and it leads to the high levels of serenity. It is a thing of beauty just as surely as the hunger and thirst after belief. It is a law of life.

I think, if I were asked to name the qualities in the poetry of our time that are both new and very vital, I should mention next, after the wider sympathy that draws all creation together into one brotherhood of living, the emergence of humor as a serious element in poetry. Humor has had a place in nineteenth century literature, but it has been usually a major theme in minor verse, or a minor relief in major poetry. It has been marginal or in the nature of an interlude. It is only in our times that humor has become functional and that our poets are beginning to employ it as a part of the serious organism of their ideas. In my own work, both in prose and verse, I have always used the humorous, not as decoration, but as a vital means to seriousness. I have used it just as I have used figures of speech and analogy and description. We live every day of our lives by humor, it is one of the best comforters and encouragers we have. It is a great teacher of calmness, of truth. It is only right that it should become a part of our illumination of deepest emotion and thinking. Maybe this virtue of laughter may stand us in good stead long after some of the virtues of intellectualism, and even of intelligence, which some of our poets cultivate so assiduously, have become as archaeological as medieval allegory.

Humor is one virtue that Edwin Arlington Robinson shares completely with Robert Frost. Here, at last, our two poets are on the same solid ground. Robinson uses humor as a means to saying some of the saddest things that can be said about ourselves and our times. But it is a happy means, as Frost points out in his Introduction to *King Jasper*. Perhaps it is in the use of such a means that Robinson is at his happiest of all. His humor is American, and New England, and quietly itself. It is clean and delicate and restrained; and yet it is playful. "Let it be said," writes Frost, "at the risk of offending the humorless in poetry's train (for there are a few such): his art was more than playful; it was humorous." Rollo Brown tells of Robinson's story of the glass-eyed man who was approached by an artist for a loan. The wealthy man said he would give the artist some money if he could tell him which of his eyes was the glass eye. The young man took one look, and said it was the right one. When asked how he had been able to tell, the artist said, "I thought your right eye looked just the least bit more sympathetic." Robinson can be as downright and direct as children are in their humor:

Out of all ancient men my childhood knew
    I choose him and I mark him for the best.
Of all authoritative liars, too,
    I crown him loveliest.

. . . .

So to the sheltered end of many a year
    He charmed the seasons out with pageantry
Wearing upon his forehead, with no fear,
    The laurel of approved iniquity.

And Robinson can be the subtle and sorrowful adult in
his humor, with years of sympathy for people behind him:

"Well, Mr. Flood, we have the harvest moon
Again, and we may not have many more;
The bird is on the wing, the poet says,
And you and I have said it here before.
Drink to the bird." He raised up to the light
The jug that he had gone so far to fill,
And answered huskily: "Well, Mr. Flood,
Since you propose it, I believe I will."

. . . .

"Only a very little, Mr. Flood—
For auld lang syne. No more, sir; that will do."
So, for the time, apparently it did,
And Eben evidently thought so too;
For soon amid the silver loneliness
Of night he lifted up his voice and sang,
Secure, with only two moons listening,
Until the whole harmonious landscape rang—

"For auld lang syne." The weary throat gave out,
The last word wavered, and the song was done.
He raised again the jug regretfully
And shook his head, and was again alone.
There was not much that was ahead of him,

And there was nothing in the town below—
Where strangers would have shut the many doors
That many friends had opened long ago.

So Mr. Flood. This is one of the tenderest studies in the human and the humorous that poetry can show. And it is one that could never have been outside of the twentieth century and outside of New England. This is E. A. at his saddest and happiest. And greatest.

I think it is significant of something very broad and vital in the history of sympathy that one of Robinson's best poems and one of Frost's are both about a drunken man who is going home alone and has to manage his destiny for himself!

Frost's humor is a poetic principle, too, and like Robinson's, a principle of life. It is also American. It is often like Mark Twain's. There is a whole-hearted boisterousness about it. But there are also reticences and reservations. Frost is a Mark Twain in fewer words. And the words omitted are New England ones. Understatement is a part of the serious business. *Litotes* might be defined as the New England quality in writing. Frost allows for the wind. He takes the wind out of big sails. He takes people down from their high horse. But he also invests them in a kind of dignity—as does Robinson—once they are down. More than dignity, sometimes—a kind of substitute for godhead! Brown, the farmer who slipped down the icy mountain, has something of that, on his way down:

> Sometimes he came with arms outspread
> Like wings, revolving in the scene

Upon his longer axis, and
    With no small dignity of mien.

Brown has very much of that peculiar godhead, after he
has brought up at the bottom:

. . . Now he snapped his eyes three times;
    Then shook his lantern, saying, "Ile's
'Bout out!" and took the long way home
    By road, a matter of several miles.

But there is no isolating Frost's humor. It is too much
a part of most of his best poems. It is like trying to
study a swallow's wing-feathers—to study Frost's quality
of humor—without the swallow attached to them. This
man's humor is a unison of life and laughter.

Such, then, are some of the rules of thumb which Frost
has worked out, for his own peace as a poet, and is so
willing to share with other people as some ways of getting
to salvation. Frost believes in little wholes that add up to
great wholesomeness. His poems are often small parcels
of little goods, at first sight; but they total up to very
massive precepts. That old-fashioned word is the best,
for this poetry so disarmingly simple and apparently so
concerned with small objects and observations. A great
part of Frost's greatness is greatness of heart and good
nature. He is sometimes like the man in his own poem
who tries to put his arms around too much. And for that
reason, at times, he has been hurt by critics who believe
most in abstract poetry and poetry in the abstract.

Robinson's greatness is of the heart, too, and of the
head. He is a good Samaritan, as well as Frost, in his in-

terest in all kinds of people. He is attracted to the weaklings and the failures, to men caught like his Cavender in the mire of a modern kind of bestiality; he is interested in old men who no longer count, and in worthless young men who never will. He writes without sentimentality and with great insight and charity. There has not often been such a balance in poetry before. Robinson believes in life even though it is full of futility and despair. He is the Sophocles of the vast private battles in the dark, the battles without trumpets and with none of the old gods looking on, battles with the issue of life or death, or, even worse, the issue of a modern kind of unkingly sanity or an unprophetic and purposeless insanity. He is a Sophocles of modern life, without the stage that was like an altar to the ancient Greeks.

It is good to have these two poets' opinions of each other. Robinson was brief in his expressed opinions. But he told Rollo Brown, his friend, once when he had been told that Frost admired his work, that all he could say was that the feeling was mutual. We have seen how Frost chose Robinson's humor in his *King Jasper* Introduction as one of the qualities of the man to praise most. He has more to say in a recent letter he wrote me: "We two were close akin up to a certain point of thinking. He would have trusted me to go a good way in speaking for him particularly on the art of poetry. We only parted company over the badness of the world. He was cast in the mold of sadness. I am neither optimist nor pessimist." And Frost adds two of his homely figures of speech that make him and his poetry so humanly alive: "I never voted either ticket. If there is a universal unfitness and unconformity as of a buttoning so started that every button on the vest is in the wrong button hole and the one empty button hole at the top and the one naked button at the bottom so far apart they have no hope of getting together, I don't care to decide whether God did this for the fun of it or for the devil of it. The two expressions come to practically the same thing anyway. Then again I am not the Platonist Robinson was. By Platonist I mean one who believes what we have here is an imperfect copy of what is in heaven." Frost goes on to apply his point in another practical metaphor, in connection with Robinson's *Tristram*: "The woman you have is an imperfect copy of some woman in heaven or in some one else's bed. Many of the world's greatest—maybe all of them—have been ranged on that romantic side. I am philosophically opposed to having one Iseult for my vocation and another for my avocation; as you may have inferred from a poem called *Two Tramps in Mud Time*. You see where that lands me on the subject of Dante's Beatrice. Mea culpa. Let me not sound the least bit smug. I define a difference with proper humility. A truly gallant Platonist will remain a bachelor as Robinson did from unwillingness to reduce any woman to the condition of being used without being idealized."

One thing that Frost admired especially about Robinson was his choosing griefs, instead of grievances, to write about. That distinction tells as much about Frost as it does about Robinson. Robert Frost is a man who has been acquainted with griefs, as he has been one acquainted with the night and day and the seasons of the year. But he doesn't lay it on his griefs for the fact that his head has grown gray. He doesn't blame it on care. He lays it on natural law, on time:

> Grief may have thought it was grief.
> Care may have thought it was care.
> They were welcome to their belief,
> The over important pair.
>
> No, it took all the snows that clung
> To the low roof over his bed,
> Beginning when he was young,
> To induce the one snow on his head.
>
> But whenever the roof came white
> The head in the dark below
> Was a shade less the color of night
> A shade more the color of snow.
>
> Grief may have thought it was grief.
> Care may have thought it was care.
> But neither one was the thief
> Of his raven color of hair.

This is a great poem for an older man to write. It is a natural poem for Robert Frost to write.

Man has trouble, and gets over it. Gets over it by believing. And goes on. That is the only way for a man who wants to live by the lifetime, and the after-lifetime, as Robert Frost wants to. I should like to close these lectures with one of Frost's most humorous poems. It is just a brief one. The metaphor in it is a very common one. Maybe it could be called crude, by some. But the poem is as fine an illustration of the road to salvation as any parable in the *Bible*. It is a poker game. It is called *In Divés' Dive*:

> It is late at night and still I am losing,
> But still I am steady and unaccusing.
>
> As long as the Declaration guards
> My right to be equal in number of cards,
>
> It is nothing to me who runs the Dive.
> Let's have a look at another five.

It is a fine thing to have had as our neighbors and contemporaries two poets whose books our grandchildren will be reading.